Imagine All Better

"I imagine, therefore I am."

Imagine All Better

Breaking Repeating Emotional and Behavioral Patterns We All Struggle With Is Easier Than You Think

Dr. Richard Crowley & Vince Kubilus

Cover concept by Vince Kubilus

Cover graphics by Vince Kubilus

Copyright © 2012 by Richard Crowley and Vince Kubilus

All rights reserved. No part of this book may be reproduced, stored in a retrieval system, or transmitted in any form or by any means, electronic, mechanical, photocopy, recording or otherwise, without the prior written permission of the publisher.

ISBN: 0977856631
ISBN 13: 9780977856633

Published by Cahill House Publishing Company
San Francisco

Also by Richard Crowley

Therapeutic Metaphors for Children and the Child Within
Second Edition
Co-authored with Joyce C. Mills

Cartoon Magic
Co-authored with Joyce C. Mills

Sammy the Elephant & Mr. Camel
Co-authored with Joyce C. Mills

Fred Protects the Vegetables
Fred Flintstone metaphorical comic book
for abused and neglected children
Co-authored with Joyce C. Mills

Mentalball: Beat Your Invisible Opponent at Its own Game
Contains some fifty stories of baseball and softball players who overcame "the yips"

Is the Pope Catholic!?!
The Catholic Nostalgia Game
A humorous and respectful pre-Vatican II board game that mixes trivia with nostalgia co-created with John Paul Crowley

We dedicate this book to Carl Jung, upon whose shoulders we stand.

*"Who looks outside, dreams.
Who looks inside, awakens."*

— Carl Jung

Carl Gustav Jung was a Swiss psychiatrist and psychotherapist who developed many current therapeutic ideas between 1900 and 1959. The groundbreaking work of Jung has provided a much-needed bridge between ancient and modern thought – between the Eastern masters and modern-day psychologists, between Western religions and modern-day seekers. At the cornerstone of Jung's framework is the *symbol*. Symbols, like metaphors, represent or suggest something beyond their immediate appearance. Jung believed that symbols mediated the entire landscape of our psychic life. The lowest to the highest aspects of the "Self" are made manifest through the use of symbols.

About the Authors

VINCE KUBILUS AND Richard Crowley are co-developers of Imagine All Better™, a life-changing, "stress-relief-on-demand" mobile app that can be installed on your iPhone, iPad, Android, tablet, and Kindle. Imagine All Better™ taps into an innate intelligence you may not be aware of, found in your right brain hemisphere where your emotions, intuition, imagination, and unconscious mind reside. The app is designed to identify and permanently remove the sources of your upsetting emotional feelings and unwanted behaviors located in your unconscious mind. More information about the app can be found on www.ImagineAllBetter.com. The authors can be reached at info@ImagineAllBetter.com.

Vince Kubilus holds an advanced degree in aerospace engineering and an MBA in finance. During his career he has worked in a wide range of fields that included solid-state physics, software design, international coproduction, process reengineering, corporate mergers and acquisitions, and administrative management. He has had a long interest in energy flows in living organisms and used classical and quantum physics principles to develop and use methods for identifying and removing impediments in energy pathways. Since 2001, he has brought benefits to individuals by removing resistances and blocks to energy flows that manifest in feelings of anxiety, frustration, self-doubt, worry, pessimism, self-blame, unworthiness, etc.

Richard Crowley has a PhD in clinical psychology. His professional training includes an internship and a Fellowship at Harvard University's primary medical and psychiatric teaching institutions. He has lectured internationally and appeared countless times in the media including USA Today, Los Angeles Times, Penthouse, NPR, the Charlie Rose Show, the Merv Griffin Show and ESPN. He served in the army as a Captain in the Medical Service Corps. Dr. Crowley has authored five books including *Mentalball: Beat Your Invisible Opponent at Its Own Game*. He is world-renowned as the originator in 1983 of a cure for helping athletes, especially baseball players and golfers, to quickly overcome a debilitating disconnect known as "the Yips".

Table of Contents

Section One

Patterns and You

	About the Authors · ix
	Introduction: Patterns and Their Operations · · · · · · · · · · · 3
Chapter 1	Why the Apple Doesn't Fall Too Far from the Tree · · · · · · · 7
	Why You Dance and What to Do About It · · · · · · · · · · · 14
Chapter 2	Who Am I? · 16
	Forty Years of Depression All Better · · · · · · · · · · · · · · · · · 19
Chapter 3	What Patterns Are Doing to You · · · · · · · · · · · · · · · · · · · 22
	Destroying Patterns · 26
	Nightmares All Better · 27
	Anatomy of a Pattern · 27
Chapter 4	Benefits of Being Free of Patterns · · · · · · · · · · · · · · · · · · 29
	How to Know When It's a Pattern or You in Control · · · · · 30
	Pain All Better · 31

Section Two

Patterns in Your Life

Chapter 5	What Patterns Do · 37
	What Patterns Do to Your Thinking · · · · · · · · · · · · · · · · 38

| | David Found His Brother's Spirit All Better · · · · · · · · · · · 39 |
| | Together Again All Better · 45 |

Chapter 6   How a Pattern Defends Itself · · · · · · · · · · · · · · · · · · 47

Chapter 7   Patterns Determine How You Interpret and
            React to Situations · 50
            Queen of Picking and Choosing
            My Battles All Better · 52

Chapter 8   Patterns and Thought Clutter · · · · · · · · · · · · · · · · · · 59

Chapter 9   Patterns and Stories · 63
            Laura's Fear of Flying All Better · · · · · · · · · · · · · · · · · 66
            Anxiety All Better · 68

Chapter 10 Intellect and Imagination · 70
            Feeling Trapped During Pregnancy All Better · · · · · · · · · 73

Chapter 11 The Origins of Patterns · 78
            First Grader Being Bullied All Better · · · · · · · · · · · · · 79
            Fear of Men All Better · 81
            Veteran's Post Traumatic Stress All Better · · · · · · · · · · 83

Chapter 12 Patterns' Unlimited Activities · · · · · · · · · · · · · · · · · 86
            How Patterns Affect the Body · · · · · · · · · · · · · · · · · · · 87
            Justin's Asperger's Manifestation All Better · · · · · · · · · 89

Chapter 13 Pattern Interactions · 92
            Individual Pattern Interactions · · · · · · · · · · · · · · · · · · 95
            Making Cold Calls All Better · · · · · · · · · · · · · · · · · · · 99
            Suggestions Cannot Change a Pattern · · · · · · · · · · · · · 101

Chapter 14 Social Media: A Feeding Frenzy for Patterns · · · · · · · · · ·103
            Distractions, Text Messaging and Bad
            Grades All Better ·106
            Surfing Porn Addiction All Better· · · · · · · · · · · · · · · · · ·107
            Enslaved by Emails All Better ·108
            Patterns and Privacy ·110
            It Chooses, Not You ·112

Chapter 15 Free Will, Free Choice and Patterns · · · · · · · · · · · · · · · 113
            Getting off the Patterns' Coins· · · · · · · · · · · · · · · · · · · 116
            Social Anxiety and Panic Attacks All Better · · · · · · · · · · · 118

Section Three
What You Need To Destroy Patterns

Chapter 16 Patterns Use Your Discomfort· 123
            What Will Work ·125
            What Won't Work ·126
            Income Tax Procrastination All Better· · · · · · · · · · · · · · · 127

Chapter 17 An Overview of How to Destroy Patterns· · · · · · · · · · · · · 130
            A really Simple Demonstration · 131
            What This Really Simple Demonstration Shows You · · · · 131

Section Four
How to Destroy Patterns

Chapter 18 How to Destroy Patterns· 133
            Step 1. Telling the 'Story':· 137
            Step 2. Rating the Story's Emotional Intensity:· · · · · · · · · 138
            Out of the Ashes and All Better · · · · · · · · · · · · · · · · · · · 139
            Step 3: Lighting up the Person's Central Pathway:· · · · · · · 141
            Step 4: Using the Imagination: · 145

Chapter 19 The Power of Imagination · 148
            Accessing the Imagination's Wisdom for
            Achieving Balance · 149
            Asking the Imagination · 151
            The Imagination's Answers · 153
            Misguided Images and Educating Images · · · · · · · · · · · · 155
            The Dating Game All Better · 158

Chapter 20 Wanted Dead or Dead-Dead:
            Ten Universal Patterns Found in Your Unconscious · · · · · 163
            Ten Universal Patterns · 164
                Nothing Response · 164
                Accusatory · 165
                Misery Loves Company · 165
                Fun · 165
                It's My Job · 165
                Power & Control · 166
                Kill & Destroy · 166
                Indifference · 166
                Parasite · 166
                Attitude · 166
            A Lifetime of Being Bullied All Better · · · · · · · · · · · · · · · · 167
            Crystal's Follow-Up · 169

Chapter 21 Annihilation Technique · 174
            Different Ways to Kill Patterns · 176
            What Not to Do When Destroying an Image · · · · · · · · · · 178
            The Skeptic · 179

Ending Statement · 181

Appendix A:
Partial Listing of Patterns That Manipulate Your Life · · · · · 183

Appendix B:
Applications of the Imagine All Better · · · · · · · · · · · · · · · · 191

Acknowledgements

We wish to express out sincere gratitude and appreciation to the clients and friends whose rich imaginations guided us to discover and learn about another world within our right brain hemisphere containing the *source* for overcoming life's obstacles we all struggle with.

In particular we gratefully acknowledge the major contributions of Jane Frizzell, who relentlessly kept us to task. Others whose invaluable feedback made the book what it is today include Kathleen Bullard, John Paul Crowley, Sean Crowley, Art Herrera, Carl Hammerschlag, Judy Kubilus, Rick Llewellyn, Joyce C. Mills, Tina Naughton Powers, Anne Pyron and Gail Sebern.

Section One

Patterns and You

*"Again and again some people in the crowd wake up.
They have no ground in the crowd,
And they emerge according to much broader laws.
They carry strange customs with them
And demand room for bold gestures.
The future speaks ruthlessly through them."*

— Rainer Maria Rilke, poet

Introduction

Patterns and Their Operations

> "The experience of transformation is therefore a kind of remembering; a remembering of our true condition, which we have forgotten."
>
> — MICHAEL GREENWOOD AND PETER NUNN

YOU CAN RELATE to the following example if a flame or a hot object has ever burned you.

Remember your reaction to coming in contact with a flame or a hot object. You pulled away from it instantly and you may have been unfortunate to be left with a wound from your encounter. The next time you found yourself in the presence of a flame or a hot object you were very wary of approaching the source of your pain. You didn't have to think about the consequences of touching the heat source; your reaction was now automatic.

However, we do learn to respond properly to various sources of heat. We use flames or hot objects to cook, heat our homes, heat water for bathing, refine petroleum and ores, and weld metals. We burn fuel in engines that propel automobiles, aircraft, ships and all kinds of useful vehicles. If we had the same fearful reaction to being burned by a flame or hot object and never developed any proper responses to various forms of heat, then we would not have the benefits of modern civilization. Obviously, this is an extreme example to the reaction to an unpleasant circumstance of being burned.

The important aspect in this example is that whenever we encounter a heat source we react immediately, without thinking, with a certain sense of fear. But the flame or hot object is not the source of that fear. The source of that fear is a "bit of energy" that attaches itself to the memory of our encounter with the heat source. The function of this bit of energy, which is called a pattern, is to protect us from burning ourselves again in a similar situation.

As you will read further on in this book, a pattern is a "form of energy" that gets encoded into our genes and passed down to our children. (You can also think of a pattern in terms of a virus that enters a cell and is activated when conditions are right for the virus' well being, not the cell's well being.) This represents a way for valuable information to be passed down to future generations as a shortcut to learning and keeping us safe from danger. Examples of common patterns are those that generate our innate fear of insects, snakes, and large animals. The reason is that many of these things can be poisonous or dangerous. Previous generations learned these lessons and succeeding generations do not have to go through the same learning process.

Now consider everyday examples of feeling fear, anxiety, worry, anger, confusion, etc. that we experience when we deal with a particular person, group of people, event or situation in our lives. You know the ones: taking a test and "blanking out", fearing to speak in front of the group, being suddenly unable to perform an athletic move, asking for what you want, having someone consistently "push your buttons", being bullied, having a series of bad relationships, to name just a few.

In each of these cases, you react automatically, without thinking, to a circumstance that you automatically blame for your upsetting feelings and unwanted behavior. Later you probably asked, "What got into me?", "Why did I do or say that thing?", or said, "What I should have said or done was…"

But your focus is on the external stimulus for your reaction and on a desire to avoid that upsetting feeling that automatically appeared. You never question what source <u>really</u> causes that upsetting feeling in the first place.

The source of your reaction is the same thing as the reaction to being burned by the hot object. A pattern, most likely inherited from your ancestors, is the real source of your discomfort. Any situation that has even some small similarity to the original memory triggers the pattern's action. The pattern, the source of your discomfort, is 'protecting' you from a perceived threatening situation by giving you a warning in the form of unpleasant feelings. However, a pattern does not, and cannot, think. A pattern reacts the same way to every triggering situation, even when the feeling and behavior it produces are a mismatch for what is really happening. Until the repeating pattern is destroyed, you will continue to react to situations and individuals in the same repeating way as if you were a robot or a vending machine.

You can be present in the moment after you destroy a pattern and enjoy freedom from its operations. Being present in the moment allows you to choose from options as opposed to unknowingly obeying a pattern's dictates. Much like the example of the proper uses of fire and heat, you will be able to choose the proper response instead of reacting predictably to a given circumstance.

The great news about a pattern's destruction is that once a pattern is destroyed, it can never return. Its destruction is permanent and irreversible. The reason is that a pattern is formed from a "then" moment in time under a specific "then" set of circumstances. No moment, no matter how minutely it is measured, can be exactly repeated or duplicated. No set of circumstances, no matter how finely defined, can be exactly duplicated. The "then" moment and the "then" set of circumstances that produced the pattern existed in the historic "then" moment, which is gone forever. Therefore, once a pattern is destroyed it is gone forever because it is literally impossible to duplicate a pattern using the "now" current moment and the "now" circumstances.

The following chapters provide detailed descriptions of how patterns operate, scientific evidence for their existence, illustrations of how they work against individual and group interests and, most importantly, how to destroy them permanently.

Imagine All Better offers you freedom.

1

Why the Apple Doesn't Fall Too Far from the Tree

"Every person has the same potential for inner tranquility, but negative forces such as fear, suspicion, greed, and hatred of one's self and others destroy inner peace."

— His Holiness the 14th Dalai Lama

WHAT IF YOU are not, nor have ever been, the author of your emotional outbursts and embarrassing or shameful behaviors? What if your addictions, shyness, procrastination, fears, worries, depressed moods, need to be perfect, and difficult interactions with others are not mental or psychological in nature, but part of the human condition you inherited genetically from your parents, grandparents, great grandparents, all the way back in time?

And what if you could permanently remove these inherited repeating patterns that run you? And each time you removed a pattern, anything else related to those particular patterns would simultaneously and permanently be removed as well?

And what if you could protect your children from going through what you, your parents and family members have adversely and painfully experienced during their lives? Well, finally you can, but in a way you have never thought about. Nobody has, until now.

Have you ever heard your parents telling each other that the older they get, the more they are becoming like their mother or father, and not in a favorable way? Yet, there is nobody to blame as your parents inherited their emotional responses and behaviors from their parents just like you inherited yours from them, and will pass it on to your offspring until this generational cycle is ended.

And even if you told yourself growing up that you would never treat your children like your parents treated you, you may unwittingly find yourself years later completely unaware of behaving like your parents, as their genetically inherited pattern has become ingrain in you unintentionally - much to your dismay.

Until now, everyone has been looking for a logical, rational reason why you and I act and think in ways that are counterproductive to our best intentions. However, a pattern cannot be "understood" because it operates in the irrational, illogical, right brain hemisphere where cause and effect have no meaning and thus cannot be "understood". In the realm of the right brain, we deal with images like a dreamscape; images are symbolic and cannot be truly understood because they are neither this nor that but something else that lies in between. Logic cannot address and get rid of patterns since patterns reside in our unconscious, outside of our conscious awareness. How can you understand what is unconscious to you, what is invisible to you? The authors offer a proven way of addressing and manifesting these patterns that press our buttons and manipulate us without needing to understand, or analyze, what they mean - ever.

You may *think* you have gotten rid of a pattern as some behavior or way of perceiving people or situations appear to have disappeared, but the pattern has not disappeared. It is still alive and will ignite your upsetting emotions of fear, frustration or anxiety in other seemingly unrelated areas of your life.

Patterns are inherited from countless generations. They are transformed from the brain into the genome, allowing them to be passed on to later generations. Dr. Barbara McClintock was awarded the 1983 Nobel Prize in Medicine and Physiology showing that genes migrate along DNA strands in response to stress. The December 2013 issue of *Nature Neuroscience* contains an article by Drs. Diaz and Ressler that show mice can pass on learned information by inheriting the traumatic or stressful memories and the response to the situation that is similar to the traumatic memory of their parents. This is an example of a pattern, a "bit of energy", that attaches itself to a memory. During the tests, the researchers presented a mouse with a cherry blossom smell. Later they introduced electrical stimulation on the mouse's rear leg simultaneously with the cherry blossom smell. After repeating this experiment numerous times, the moment the mouse smelled the cherry blossom, it became nervous, anxious and fearful knowing it was going to be zapped again. Then they tested this mouse's first generation offspring, his "children", but none of them were given any electrical stimulation when they were introduced to the same cherry blossom smell. However, upon being introduced to that same smell given their "father", they all became nervous, anxious and fearful. And the same anxiety-provoking results occurred to their own offspring, the original mouse's "grandchildren".

Research in *Nature Neuroscience* demonstrated that traumatic situations can affect the DNA of sperm cells, going so far as to change the brains, and the behavior of succeeding generations. According to a British Broadcasting Corporation (BBC) report, the study concludes that, "The experiences of a parent, even before conceiving, markedly influence both structure and function in the nervous system of subsequent generations."

Although this result has not been confirmed in humans, scientists conclude it seems reasonable to assume that we exhibit similar inherited phobias, depression, anxieties, compulsions, anger, etc. Look at your emotional reactions - or lack of them - and then look at your parent's behaviors and emotional reactions with you and others. Some of them see the glass half full, others half empty; some have what you perceive as "irrational", "neurotic" fears and anxieties; others are hypercritical and may be prone to yell; others don't get you no matter how hard you try to get them to do so. And if you can engage your parents to recollect their parents' reactions and emotions displayed to them growing up, you will see the generational patterns orchestrating your grandparents, your parents - and you. It appears that nature has given all living things a mechanism by which future generations would automatically know how to behave - through the automatic operations of patterns - when those generations encountered similar situations, even if that behavior is not in our best interests. We rarely encounter threats to our lives from wild animals or hostile humans during our modern lives.

It is these patterns that cause us to behave automatically in certain situations. Automatic behaviors are centered in the unconscious right brain, which performs an extremely valuable function by taking over repetitive actions and allow us to identify the unique aspects of our environment. Consider how complex your average day would be if you had to consciously think about every individual action you took – from eating, bathing, getting dressed to using a phone to getting to and from a school, workplace or appointment. Once a repetitive action has been learned, the right brain takes over and you do it without much, if any, thought. A pattern, which is inherited or can be acquired, triggers an automatic behavior or response. That pattern resides in the unconscious right brain where it operates as it did when it first originated during some distant historical event.

Human history - Western, Eastern, African, Native American or Pacific Islander - is a story of war, famine, plague, enslavement, persecution, pestilence, forced migration and brutality. The peace that we collectively seek is like the small set of punctuation marks in a long turbulent narrative. In summary, history is a story of upsetting, traumatic events in both societal and individual family settings.

And those familial and societal traumatic memories are passed down through the millennia to us, in whom upsetting behaviors and reactions are automatically triggered by perceptions that lie in the unconscious right brain – the same part of the brain where emotions, intuition, imagination and the unconscious reside. Various forms of talk therapy are the tools that are used to identify and remedy the causes of upsetting behaviors. However, conventional talk therapy is an analytical tool of the conscious left brain that does not operate where the upsetting behaviors and reactions originate – in the right brain. Using an analytical tool to permanently delete an upsetting behavior is like looking for a lost set of keys under a street light on a dark night simply because that is where the light is better, even though you dropped the keys in a distant field.

Until now, there was no way to shine the street light on the field in the very spot where the keys were dropped. That is, there was no practical, effective tool that would permanently and easily destroy the *source*, or the pattern, responsible for the upsetting behavior. This book describes what those patterns are, how they begin, how they operate and, most importantly, how they can be permanently destroyed. In doing so, you will avoid passing those genetically inherited sources, or repeating patterns, on to your children and their children, ad infinitum. You will also learn how destroying those patterns within you will bring benefit not only to yourself but also to all those around you with no conscious effort on your part.

Because inherited patterns operate in the unconscious, where they remain out of conscious awareness, each generation acts out the patterns' blueprints without knowing why. Everyone has known the feeling of being "taken over by something" in situations where they acted in ways that were clearly not in their best interests. As a result, everyone tries harder – athletes focus on their "mechanics", students study longer, actors do affirmations, etc. – but their left-brain conscious focus can never be where the left brain can't go, which is the right-brain unconscious. All the conscious effort to get rid of the upsetting behaviors and feelings will produce only temporary relief at best. The unconscious patterns are left intact.

And so each generation adds its energy to the patterns with the upsetting feelings that arise when patterns operate and cause us to perceive and react to situations through the patterns' filters. Although everyone benefits when patterns are destroyed, the younger an individual is when a pattern is destroyed, the greater the benefit that the individual will enjoy in terms of improved relationships throughout life and the enhanced quality of that life. The next generation will benefit from the absence of the patterns that their parents destroyed and never passed on.

Since the "sins of the fathers" are the inherited patterns, they can be erased forever. Those inherited patterns are not yours to endure; they are not who you are. Just as you cannot identify yourself as a physical virus that causes you physical distress, you cannot identify yourself with a pattern, this "psychic virus", this "invisible opponent" that causes you uncontrollable upsetting feelings and unwanted repeating behaviors with certain people, situations or life in general. Until now, nearly everyone has bought into the false beliefs authored by the patterns that dictate: "I am my worst enemy; I sabotage myself; I make bad choices; I, and I alone, am totally responsible."

The authors have developed a life-changing, "stress-relief-on-demand" mobile app that can be installed on your iPhone, iPad, Android, tablet, and Kindle. The app allows you, family members and friends to be walked through a process in your imagination to eliminate these inherited pattens. The more patterns eliminated, the quieter and less cluttered your mind becomes and the more present and aware you are with yourself and your environment.

Imagine All Better is for informational purposes only. It is not intended to diagnose, prescribe or treat, and is not care nor a substitute for care from a licensed healthcare professional; nor is it intended to replace the care, services or treatments of a licensed healthcare professional. You should consult a licensed healthcare professional in all matters related your physical and mental health, and particularly in respect to your concerns or any symptoms that may require diagnosis or medical attention.

- Anxiety (Fears, negative thoughts, worries about "what if", what I coulda, shoulda, woulda said or done)
- Blocks to creative processes (Actors, composers, fine artists, musicians, writers, etc.)
- Bugged/Controlled by people who press my buttons (Children, parents, teachers, politicians, coaches, friends, coworkers, spouses/partners, etc.)
- Bullied/Cyberbullied/Made fun of or put down/Picked on (School, neighborhood, workplace, siblings, bosses, relationships, marriages, in-laws, etc.
- "Character flaws" (Feeling inadequate, shame, incomplete, scarred, defective, "damaged", etc.)
- Fighting/wrestling with my demons
- Financial worries
- Health concerns (Reduce intensity of emotional feelings associated with medical symptoms, diagnoses, waiting for test results, flus, colds, etc., unable to do what is in my best interest)
- I'm my worst enemy/I sabotage myself
- Insecurities/Confidence issues
- Making the same mistakes I swore I'd never make again
- No matter what I do, it's never good enough/Always disappointing others
- Parenting skills (Worried about being a good parent)
- Relationship problems (Always finding losers, bad breakups, betrayed, taken advantage of, etc.)
- School issues (Test anxiety, social standing, bored, underachieving, "lazy", etc.)
- Sports performance (Over thinking, anxiety, mad at myself, second guessing, down/depressed, body tension, physiological discomfort, etc.)

- Stress (Acute, chronic)
- Workplace interactions (Job insecurity, lack of motivation, fear of asking for a raise, anxiety about making presentations, hate cold calling, annoying coworkers, etc.)

This book offers for the first time a proven method for achieving satisfaction, peace, clarity and expanded awareness. Once the frustrating patterns that block your path to your hopes and dreams are destroyed, they can never interfere in your life again. Never!

You will learn exactly what prevents you from achieving your hopes and dreams, and you will learn precisely how to destroy the patterns that are controlling you rather than merely coping with them. Destroying a pattern results in your freedom from its operation, which allows you to be present in the moment. Being in the moment allows you to choose from options as opposed to unknowingly obeying a pattern's dictates.

Why You Dance and What to Do About It

People cling tightly to the notions of who they *think* they are and how the world is supposed to work. People identify themselves as their egos, not the pure awareness that allows them to have their perceptions in the first place. Anything that threatens the notion of self is perceived as a threat to their physical existence, i.e. death. We live in an age of accelerating technological and philosophical changes, which threaten cherished assumptions of "how things are supposed to be". People want to hold on to something for a sense of stability, and a reassurance that they will continue to exist. But, as you read in the preceding section, "Who Am I", there is no thing, nothing, to cling to – every thing, without exception, changes, including our perceptions and applications of the "truth".

Your ego is a combination of who you *think* you are and your *interpretation* of how the world is supposed to work. Advertising, entertainment and political figures use their understanding of our egos to achieve their goals. Advertising that appears to provide a solution to some fear, such as a fear of disease, can be highly effective. Illusionists use diversion and optical illusions to entertain us with magic tricks that seem to defy reality. Politicians appeal to a fear of chaos by representing themselves and their ideas as a way to maintain and increase control over future events and thereby keep us safe from the threat and the opposition party.

The patterns within you keep you focused on situations, events, behaviors and stories that are outside yourself. You react to that external input in a way that is determined by a pattern or patterns. You may feel insulted or praised, threatened or comforted by words, sounds or gestures, but those words, sounds or gestures have no meanings or emotions attached to them. Your perceptions, which give rise to your reactions, are your reality – or so you believe. And so you never question the reason why you react the way you do, and the patterns within you remain safely hidden, operating in the unconscious of your right brain – totally removed from the awareness in your left rational brain.

As a result, people go through life in a trance doing a dance that is choreographed by an assembly of shared patterns. Body language, words, sounds, gestures and facial expressions provoke reactions and behaviors in others, who, in turn, react and behave in predictable ways that provoke predictable reactions and behaviors in those around them. And so it goes, in families or businesses, schools or theater groups, hospitals or car dealerships – in any organization – the interactions of patterns determine the perceptions, behaviors and choices within that organization.

Imagine All Better offers you freedom.

2

Who Am I?

"We used to wonder where war lived, what it was that made it so vile. And now we realize that we know where it lives, that it is inside ourselves."

— Albert Camus

Ask yourself the question, "Who am I?" The answer will appear by eliminating all those facets of who you think you are, which is your ego, your self image, how you identify yourself. Consider the following answers that commonly come to mind:

-You are not your name. You can change your name, but you will remain who you are.
-You are not your position in a family. You can leave your family or be placed with another family shortly after your birth, but you will remain who you are.

- You are not your body. Your body will change as you age. You can change your appearance through surgery, lose body parts, and even change your sex, but you will remain who you are.
- You are not your professional skill, job title or financial condition. Your skill will become obsolete, you will shed your job title and your financial condition will change, but you will remain who you are.
- You are not your social status. Your social status will change, but you will remain who you are.
- You are not your possessions. Your possessions will come and go and the value you place on them will change, but you will remain who you are.
- You are not your accomplishments or the awards you receive for them. Your accomplishments and the awards will be forgotten, but you will remain who you are.
- You are not your behavior and the labels applied to it, such as hero, rescuer, Mr. Fix-It, victim, addict, neurotic, healer, drama queen, sage, liar, etc. Your behavior will change, but you will remain who you are.
- You are not your knowledge. You can always learn more about any subject, find that your knowledge is wrong, and forget what you know, but you will remain who you are.
- You are not your understanding or wisdom. Like everything else, your understanding and wisdom will continuously change, but you will remain who you are.
- You are not your likes, dislikes, aversions, talents, intelligence or memory. All of those will change, but you will remain who you are.

But "Who Am I?" The answer is, You Are Pure Awareness. So why do individuals and organizations ignore warning signals, disregard sound advice, make bad choices and behave in ways that are clearly not in their best interests? The answer is the operations of the patterns within the right brain, the realm of the unconscious. Until you destroy the patterns that limit you, you can never perceive or think "outside the box", because that box is constructed and maintained by patterns. No amount of external action, speaking or wishing can destroy a pattern, which is a highly manipulative, internal opponent.

This book describes what patterns are, where they come from and how they operate. Most importantly, you will learn how to destroy any pattern quickly, easily and permanently and replace it with supportive, balancing energy. You may be left with the memory of a person, group, event or situation but without the associated upsetting feeling. You will find a newfound peace of mind and freedom to choose. You will be surprised to discover that you have been dancing to a pattern's music all along.

In this Section One, you will learn that everyone has patterns within them and what patterns are doing to your life.

In Section Two, you will learn what patterns are, how they enter your unconscious, how they operate, and how they order your 'reality' by limiting your perceptions.

In Section Three, you will learn specifically how to shut off your negative or anxious thoughts whenever you wish and enjoy relief from the turmoil of inner chatter.

In Section Four, you will learn the infinite capability of your imagination, which you control completely, and can use to destroy patterns. You will learn specific steps for destroying patterns and replacing them with energies that serve you.

Our intention in writing this book is for you to become proficient and confident in helping yourself and others. The Imagine All Better process described in this book will put an end to the patterns' malicious operations on your mind and life. In summary, Imagine All Better offers you freedom.

A typical example of the dramatic effectiveness of the Imagine All Better process is the story of a woman who received great benefit from one brief session.

Forty Years of Depression All Better

I telephoned an old friend, Carolyn, whom I had not spoken with in some time. At the age of 60 she had undergone 17 surgeries that left her with a walker and in a lot of pain. Today was one of her particularly bad days. I told her that my associate and I had achieved excellent results from having developed a unique quantum physics addition to our current process with the potential to permanently delete any frustrating, upsetting emotions associated with relationships, bullies, bosses, employment, pets, children, symptoms, medical diagnoses and your hopes and dreams. Carolyn was more preoccupied with her pain and less impressed with my news.

Carolyn said, "I'm so bummed out and depressed over all the pain in my body that I had to cancel lunch with a girlfriend whom I had been looking forward to seeing." I told her that this process could easily get rid of her depressed feelings. I asked her to rate what number those feelings would be on a scale of zero-to-10 with zero being absolutely no depressed feelings and 10 being extremely depressed. She initially replied, "Nine," When asked if that was the highest number ever associated with depression in her life, Carolyn laughed and said, "Are you kidding? Whenever I feel down and hopeless being physically immobilized with pain, I find myself reliving the painful story 40 years ago of being on the psychiatric locked ward of Camarillo State Hospital in California. I thought I would never be released. So that would be a 10 plus! I've tried to push that memory back down whenever it comes to mind, but deep down inside it's never gone away. It's always in the back of my mind. I've hidden it from everyone. I've never even told my twenty-seven-year-old daughter about that hellish time. And that hospital was only one of a dozen psych hospitals I was in during that time in my life."

I asked her to focus on that particular memory that had a 10-plus emotional intensity associated with it, while I worked remotely on her central pathway in my mind. I proceeded to imagine seeing gold light illuminating from Carolyn's central pathway, which begins at the bridge of her nose, across her forehead, over the top of her head, down the back of her head and all the way down her spinal column to the tip of her tailbone – found in Chapter Eighteen. Each time I did so, I asked Carolyn to rank what number the intensity of her depression was. She began to report the numbers quickly decreasing to a seven, a five, a three, and then giggling said, "It's zero!" I asked her to intentionally bring up any lingering emotions still associated with that terrible depressing memory of her in that locked ward. Carolyn said she could not find any. Jokingly I said, "Come on now, Carolyn. Forty years of depression always in the back of your mind and you can't pull it back in?" "No!" she exclaimed while giggling even more. "What the hell did you do?"

I told her that the chronic feeling of depression that had been haunting her all these many years would never ever return. Carolyn added, "I've hated that memory. I've carried that painful memory for all these years, and now I actually feel calm. I can't believe I'm smiling while talking about having been on a psyche-ward at Camarillo State Hospital!"

As I lit up her central pathway she felt the intensity of her debilitating depression become weaker and weaker until it was gone. Gone for good. She had what we call an associated emotion that can be eliminated by the Imagine All Better process that you will learn about later. It took no more than ten minutes to give her peace of mind.

A week later, Carolyn excitedly reported, "It was a remarkable thing you did! Before I went to bed that same evening last week, I found myself continuously smiling while thinking about Camarillo State Hospital. That was a first. In the past if I had to drive north on the freeway to visit friends in Ventura, I had to drive past Camarillo and pass by that hospital. I always held onto the steering wheel ever so tightly and would even stop breathing; it was a different disturbance than I've ever experienced. It's truly amazing how years, no, how decades of pain have been lifted from this tired old body. Even breathing seems easier."

"Anything else?" I asked, knowing that this approach simultaneously affects other seemingly unrelated parts of your life. Carolyn concurred by saying, "You remember the story of how my mean and controlling mother forced me to go with her to Mexico City to have an abortion when I was 23 years old. I was petrified for the obvious reasons, but the memory of the Spanish voices of the doctors and nurses who aborted my fetus never left me. The other day my roommate, Connie, asked if I would like to go with her to Olvera Street on Saturday. You know, the historic Mexican section in downtown Los Angeles where all the Mexican shops and music are located. What came out of me before I knew it was, 'Sure. I'd love to go.' I responded so quickly without any hesitation. I was so surprised because I never allowed myself to ever *think* about "it." That was how I protected myself because anything Hispanic would trigger Mexico City. Prior to last week, I would have created an excuse to get out of going to Olvera Street. It was enlightening to not physically feel angst nor remove myself."

A couple of months later I spoke with Carolyn who had undergone yet another surgery. She said it was the easiest surgery she had ever had, and she recuperated the fastest. She reminded me that she had once weighed 367 pounds and had undergone "stomach stapling surgery" in the 1970s and gastric bypass surgery in the 1990s as she had no control over her compulsive eating. However, since the pattern of depression was annihilated, she has been relaxed for the first time in her life and said she's eating like a "normal person," able to leave food on the plate without any compulsion to finish it. She said, "That's so weird since we never discussed my weight problem, only the depression from 40 years ago."

Carolyn was correct. By working on a pattern and destroying it, this approach also benefits other seemingly unrelated issues in other areas of your life. In Carolyn's case, she experienced the easiest surgery ever, was more relaxed than she can remember, and her cravings ended. With a malicious, traumatic pattern annihilated, her emotional state spontaneously returned to a time prior to her abortion and subsequent depression as if they never happened.

Imagine All Better offers you freedom.

3

What Patterns Are Doing to You

"No matter what area of your life seems to you to be blocked or thwarted, stop and reconsider: you will recognize the outer 'enemy' as but a reflection of what you have not, before now, been willing or able to recognize as coming from within."

— RALPH BLUM, AUTHOR

PATTERNS INFLUENCE YOUR thoughts, feelings, attitudes and perceptions in order to ensure their survival at your expense. You unknowingly satisfy the patterns' bidding, which prevents you from achieving success, harmony and balance. Patterns are energy-sucking viruses that disconnect you from your peace of mind, optimism, enthusiasm, self-confidence and joy. The energy that the patterns steal from you compromises your medical, emotional and spiritual well-being. As this gap between your spirit and yourself widens, patterns become stronger by siphoning your energy. The wider the abyss, the more vulnerable you are to depressions, anxieties, addictions, broken relationships, medical symptoms, chronic pains, and even suicide and homicide.

If you have noticed any of the following repetitive behaviors or feelings in yourself, then you have experienced the results caused by patterns:

- A chronic health issue that defies diagnosis and/or treatment
- Any phobia
- Addictions and compulsive behaviors
- Constant, detrimental background feelings such as anxiety, anger, sadness, fear, shame, etc.
- Relationship difficulties with spouses, significant others, bosses, co- workers, parents, children, clients, etc.

A pattern is like a bully that intimidates your well-being. It makes you describe yourself as feeling lost, in a world of your own, disconnected, spaced out, in an altered state, not your old self, under a spell, beside yourself, confused, hopeless and blaming yourself. It ties you up with relentless guilt and pins you down with debilitating thoughts until you are caught in its vicious cycle. It makes you believe that you have created all your problems. It laughs sinisterly whenever you try to understand it through analyses and interpretations.

It makes you falsely believe: "One part of me wants to get better and another part of me doesn't." "One part of me wants to be successful while another part wants to be a failure." "One part of me wants to stop doing certain things, and another part of me doesn't." The 'part' of you that is opposed to your heart's desires is a pattern operating. Your spirit wants you to be content, healed and balanced and get on with your life. An oppositional pattern makes you believe that you are in an accusatory battle with yourself while the pattern hides in the shadows scripting all your conflicts. Any voice or thoughts in your head that does not whole-heartedly support your being successful, healthy and balanced is not the voice of your spirit. It is the voice of a pattern that, until now, has had you tricked into believing that this inner dialogue is only between yourself. A pattern in you creates inner conflict that generates upsetting emotions. While you are being emotionally beaten up during this argumentative conversation in your head, the pattern schemes its next invisible plot and trick.

A frequent chronic complaint is, "Why am I feeling tired all the time?" Such an analytical question will never regenerate your energy, but will continue to drain you further because the pattern *loves* you to go down the dead-end alley of analyzing your feelings and not looking at the source of your feeling, which is the pattern itself causing the fatigue. A pattern enslaves your mind and puts your perception to work on the pattern's own agenda. Patterns make you perceive your world the way they want you to see it, through their filters, and con you into believing it is your "reality". You then react to those perceptions in a way that drains your energy and feeds the patterns.

A nasty pattern can make you fall into painfully deep holes of despair from time to time or abandon you in never-ending shallow depressions. Then the pattern will use *your* rationale to justify reasons for your despair or depression.

Patterns make you incapable of seeing effective choices that would be readily apparent to someone else. Conscious awareness becomes an intellectual concept and no longer an obtainable commodity. Activities you would have done effortlessly in the past become a struggle or even impossible at times. Sometimes getting out of bed in the morning becomes an arduous task. As long as the pattern operates, and you blame yourself, analyze your feelings and rationalize why you feel that way, you will remain stuck.

Patterns are the puppet masters controlling you like a marionette on strings. Patterns are the puppet masters who remain invisible to your 'audience'. The only perception the puppet-show audience view as 'reality' is the behavior of the marionettes. Whatever the marionettes do, the audience accepts with applause or rejects with boos. The audience judges the observable, visible behavior of the marionette and not the unobservable, invisible behavior of the puppet master pulling your strings. The whole world is a puppet show because every human has patterns unknowingly operating at all times.

You are not the cause of your destructive behaviors on the job, in your relationships or dealing with addictions. Patterns are!

Key characteristics of patterns' behaviors are:

- Your perceptions and reactions are determined by patterns that are inherited or formed in your childhood or later years. Your behavior is controlled by the energy patterns within you. Other names for the term 'patterns' are: programs, inner conflicts, invisible opponents, wrestling with your demons, and being your own worst enemy.
- These patterns work in the unconscious, removed from your conscious awareness. Patterns cause internal mental chatter and compulsive behaviors.
- A pattern is concerned only with its survival. It disguises its presence by causing you to project and blame its operations onto others and external conditions. A pattern will allow you to see and do only those things that do not threaten its existence.
- Any action, such as continuously talking and even thinking about your problems, is motivated by your discomfort, which is caused by a pattern. But a pattern will cause you to focus on your discomfort - not the pattern itself. Since a pattern feeds on your negative emotions, talking and even thinking about your problems will only strengthen that pattern. Therefore, a pattern will become stronger every time you are *reacting*, not responding, to a situation in which the pattern operates. A *reaction* is an automatic thought, emotion or behavior in a situation that is caused by a pattern. A *response* is a pattern-free choice of a thought, emotion or behavior in a situation that is proper and appropriate to what is happening in the moment.

- A pattern does not restrict its operation to only one aspect of your life. A pattern has a ripple effect. Any single pattern affects all areas of your life because a pattern is energy, and that energy permeates your entire physical and psychological states, just like a radio wave passes though every cell of your body.

Destroying Patterns
This list of characteristics would seem to indicate that identifying and removing any pattern is a formidable task that requires great preparation and prolonged work. In fact, your reading this sentence indicates that you have the most important skills needed to neutralize a pattern: awareness, attention, and focus. Your awareness of the presence of a pattern is necessary as a first step in getting rid of it. Your continued attention, combined with the Imagine All Better process, will quickly and easily destroy any pattern so that it can never operate again. In addition, all emotions and intense feelings associated with a pattern are removed and can never return.

Imagine All Better has the potential to permanently destroy any repeating, upsetting emotions associated with your self-image, illnesses, stresses, relationships, behaviors, addictions, etc. that tend to repeat themselves throughout your life. Anyone, anywhere in the world, can learn this method. It places the entire world on the same level for being change agents who break patterns that confine us. Accepting or coping with chronic, upsetting emotions becomes a thing of the past. Our approach for removing upsetting emotions challenges the widely held belief that the past is the past and that you cannot do anything about it.

When you eradicate a pattern, you return the pattern's energy, which it was stealing from you all along, to your awareness and thereby expand your consciousness. Each pattern that you annihilate steadily adds to your ability to remain 'in the now', present to what is happening in the moment.

Nightmares All Better

All I knew about Lenny was that he was 28, unemployed, living with his family, and under a psychiatrist's care for ongoing nightmares that tormented him. The psychiatrist's use of prescription medications was ineffective and Lenny continued to have terrifying dreams that awakened him feeling angry and fearful. The psychiatrist increased Lenny's nighttime-medication strength to guarantee his sleeping all night. Lenny complied, woke up feeling drugged, and his nightmares continued. The pattern continued its feeding frenzy on Lenny's anger and fear. The psychiatrist was considering hospitalizing Lenny in a psychiatric facility for observation.

We worked together for an hour. I called him two days later to see what the results were. Lenny said, "That night following our telephone session I don't remember dreaming at all, and I woke up at 8:30 a.m. refreshed! That was the longest I have been able to sleep since I can remember. And I didn't wake up angry or scared at all."

Lenny's tormenting nightmares never returned; he never ended up in a psychiatric facility; his psychiatrist gradually took him off his medications and within a month he found a well-paying job.

Anatomy of a Pattern

Patterns' natures cause them to operate in predictable, repetitive ways. Here is a summary listing of their energetic anatomy:

- Patterns exist in the unconscious, where memories about everything that has ever happened to you in your life are stored. Patterns make use of every bit of this information to defend themselves from your attempts to recognize and destroy them.
- Although the pattern knows everything about you and will use the information to protect itself, *the pattern cannot think*. A pattern is similar to a physical virus that invades the nucleus of the cell. A virus knows how to ensure its survival and to use the nucleus to reproduce itself, but the virus, like a pattern, cannot

think. Patterns, viruses and bacteria operate on survival instinct rather than logical thought.
- The behavior of all patterns follows a predictable, repetitive and sequential path. For example, you become frustrated or angry when something does not produce an expected result. Patterns dictate that you behave in such a predictable way, which is a reaction, *not* a response.
- Patterns have only one motivation and that is their continued survival, which *always* is at the expense of your peace of mind and enjoyment of life.
- Patterns use your emotional energy to prevent you from becoming aware of their existence and interfering with their operations or destroying them.
- Every action that you take that is motivated by a pattern will strengthen the pattern. This includes talking about the pattern and resisting an emotion or feeling that is associated with the pattern. For example, avoiding or dismissing thoughts about an annoying relative, neighbor or boss will intensify and prolong the annoying feelings associated with the thoughts.
- Everything within your unconscious also operates continuously even during your physical sleep. The patterns never sleep or take any time off. Everything, including your dreams that you perceive, is filtered by the patterns' operations. You are unknowingly compelled by patterns to interpret, or rather misinterpret, what is happening and what has happened in a way that preserves or enhances the patterns' existence.

Imagine All Better offers you freedom.

4

Benefits of Being Free of Patterns

> *"What kept a person in a chronic state of illness? I saw the body composed of separate parts surrounded by walls. Somehow those parts were not being recognized by the body. Through some form of self-destructive urge, hate, or avoidance, their separate parts could not communicate with each other."*
>
> — FRED ALAN WOLF, PHYSICIST AND AUTHOR

BEING FREE OF the invisible opponent of patterns allows you to make actual choices and allows you to "be in the moment", both of which the pattern prevents. As you remove patterns, your attachments to negative people, harmful activities and accumulating unnecessary possessions disappear. In place of negative attachments, you will find detachment, that is freedom, which is your enjoyment of whatever you are doing or experiencing. However, you will have the understanding that these things cannot bring you a sense of completion or balance. *You are complete just as you are.* There is nothing outside of yourself that is necessary to complete you. And so you will become detached and free, enjoying your life fully and feeling your emotions while *knowing without thinking*.

Our culture values intellectual achievement. We prize logical thinking and hence believe our thoughts, not realizing that our thoughts are filtered by patterns. Each of us knows what to do in every moment, but the logical mind prevents us from ready access to a fitting, effective response. When you destroy the patterns that filter your thoughts, you know without thinking what the proper choice is in the moment, just as you know without thinking when your are thirsty, hungry, tired or choosing an item from a restaurant menu. In summary, when you destroy crazy-making patterns, inner conflict disappears immediately.

How to Know When It's a Pattern or You in Control

A pattern takes control of your thinking in order to convince you that the pattern is you – that you and the pattern are one. It convinces you that your 'reality' is *really* what is happening now and what has happened really did happen the way you perceived it. A pattern will use your perception and your intellect to disguise itself in three main ways: blaming, analyzing and rationalizing.

- **Blaming** yourself, a person, event or process for your feelings: A common example is the statement: "If only he/she/it would behave differently, then I would feel better." The pattern hides itself by making you talk or think about topics that are known to cause you an emotional upset. You blame someone or something for your emotional turmoil. And since the pattern's blame-game is a two-way street, and sometimes a three-way street, you find yourself blaming yourself and being blamed by others, which presses your buttons and the pattern is off and running having a field day with you and others.

- **Analyzing** a feeling: Needing to *understand* or questioning *why* you feel the way you do about an event or process cannot reveal the source of the feeling, since you are focused on the effect of the pattern, i.e. frustration, and not on the pattern itself. A common question is: "Why do I feel this way?" A rational answer cannot change the feeling. A rational answer can only strengthen a pattern because analysis keeps you in your left brain, while the conniving pattern hides in your right brain.
- **Rationalizing** your behavior: A pattern is controlling you when you hear yourself saying or thinking, "That's just the way I am", "I'm stubborn because I'm Irish", "I can't help myself", "It's my nature" or "I'm just like my parents; it runs in the family." A pattern hides behind a wall of rational plausibility frustrating your ability to perceive what is *really* happening.

Pain All Better

The following story of Sylvia shows a typical example where the combination of the imagination and lighting up the central pathway with gold light ended a pattern's control. Sylvia, age 62, began having sciatica a year and a half ago. She was in front of her computer and emailed me a description of sciatica from the Internet: "Although sciatica is a relatively common form of low back pain and leg pain, the true meaning of the term is often misunderstood. Sciatica is a set of symptoms rather than a diagnosis for what is irritating the root of the nerve, causing the pain." Outside of the fact Sylvia had lost 80 pounds in the past three years and had 20 more to reach her goal that was all I knew about her. She said she was interested in receiving relief from the sciatica, and so we began the work.

Sylvia said when the sciatica takes over she feels aggravated, and if it were no longer there she would feel a sense of peacefulness and wholeness. I had her rate the feeling of being aggravated on a zero-to-10 scale when sciatica takes over and Sylvia said it was a 10 and that it makes her shake.

I lit up her central pathway with gold light from the bridge of her nose to the tip of her tailbone, just like I did with Carolyn earlier, and she reported the next number being an eight. Instead of the number dropping to a lower one when I lit up her central pathway again, she said it was now a nine. It indicated that we needed to call upon Sylvia's imagination for an image that represented the very first time she felt aggravated.

"Sylvia, with your eyes open or closed, quietly in your mind so I don't hear it, tell your imagination, and not yourself, to give you an image, person, cartoon, monster, somebody or something that made you feel aggravated the first time ever in your life."

"It's an arrow coming toward me."

"Ask the arrow how it benefits the arrow to make you feel so aggravated."

"Its reply was, 'It makes me happy.' And the next thing it said was 'Power.'"

"It gets to be happy and powerful at your expense. Destroy it, as it's a pattern. Actually, it's two patterns in one. One of them we call a 'Parasite' as it gets to feel happy by sucking out all your happiness leaving you feeling unhappy. And the other one is what we call 'Power and Control" as this pattern's intention is to leave you powerless and out of control.

"I burned it up."

"Now ask your imagination quietly in your mind for it, and not yourself, to give you the most positive image with the most positive energy to reconnect you back to your original spirit of peacefulness and wholeness.

"It's sunshine."

"Ask it if it is here to help you feel peacefulness and wholeness."

"It comes closer to me. And I am having a warm and tingling feeling."

"Then welcome that image of the sunshine to come inside your heart, spirit and every cell in your body. Double-check to see if there's any doubt or skepticism for that image being here to help you feel peacefulness and wholeness again."

"None whatsoever."

"Okay. Let's return to the scale of zero-to-10 scale and your memory of feeling aggravated associated with the pain increasing that makes you shake."

As I remotely imagined lighting up her central pathway with gold light several more times, Sylvia's previous number of a nine eventually dropped to a two, yet stayed there and would not budge. So I had her enlist her imagination again to come up with an image, a person, a monster or a cartoon figure that kept her disconnected from being at peace and serene and had her ask it what its purpose was.

"It's a skeleton face and when I asked its purpose, it stuck its tongue out."

"That's one of the patterns called an 'Attitude'. As long as it's there, it's causing your problem. Zap it! Destroy it!"

"I put it down the garbage disposal."

"Your imagination always needs to see the complete destruction of the pattern's symbolic image right in front of you. That pattern is rather upset with what we're doing as it lives off of upsetting emotions and unwanted behaviors, and will do anything to maintain its existence. Like a trickster, it just played a game on you by having you believe you finally got rid of it in the garbage disposal knowing very well it is not destroyed, and it will continue to create your problem."

"Okay. I've pulverized it with a mortar and pestle. It's destroyed now."

When she asked her imagination for a positive image to feel peaceful and serene, her imagination gave her an image of the sun. Initially, there was no skepticism of the sun's image being here to help until she said, "Well, I do have a little fear. Last week, my mother had a stroke and my sciatica increased upon hearing it."

I told her to have her imagination present her an image that generated the sciatica associated with hearing about her mother's stroke and an image of a person standing behind her holding an umbrella appeared immediately. Since the person had no intention of removing the fear, she believed she annihilated it by putting it down the drain.

"That's the pattern again trying to trick you into believing that you can't get rid of it Sylvia. I have an idea. Pretend you can click your heels together and imagine the person with the umbrella turning into a fragile glass figurine of itself and a boulder falling out of the sky on top of it and smashing it."

"The minute I did that my current pain disappeared as well."

"Now have your imagination, and not you, give you the most positive image with the most positive energy that truly reconnects you to feel peaceful and serene."

"It's a conga line of colorful parrots. You know, the ones on TV in the commercial about Margaritaville and parrots."

"I'm all too familiar with margaritas, but not with the commercial. Ask the image if it is here to reconnect you to feel at peace and serene, now and in the future."

"Yes. The parrots are now singing and dancing in a conga line all around me. I feel great!"

"Welcome that image to come inside your heart, your spirit and every cell in your body. The image will know what to do."

"Any skeptic or doubt for that image?"

"None. I just feel really good."

"So go back to that original upsetting memory on a zero-to-10 scale and see what number it is now."

"I can't pull in any number. I have a circle of protection around me, and I don't hurt either."

Imagine All Better offers you freedom.

Section Two

Patterns in Your Life

"We too can become dissociated and lose our identity. We can be possessed and altered by moods, or become unreasonable and unable to recall important facts about ourselves or others, so that people ask: "What the devil has got into you? We talk about being able "to control ourselves," but ...self-control is a rare and remarkable virtue. We may think we have ourselves under control; yet a friend can easily tell us things about ourselves of which we have no knowledge."

— Carl Jung

5

What Patterns Do

"To adhere to an outmoded belief system is like carrying the raft after you have crossed the water."

— Buddhist saying

How many times have you asked yourself, "I know better than doing what I did. Why did I do it? What possessed me to do that?" Or, "What the hell got into me to lose control and get so upset?" Then you hear yourself reply, "I don't know." Of course you don't know; you will *never* know, because you are seeking a logical answer to an illogical motivation – one that is beyond the reach of space, time, reasoning, cause-and-effect and even personal responsibility. Patterns within you have hijacked your perceptions, reactions and sense of responsibility by making you believe that your version of 'reality' is what is really happening.

Merriam-Webster defines responsibility as "answerable or accountable, as for something *within* one's power, control, or management….

chargeable with being the *author, cause,* or occasion of something… capable of *rational* thought or action." A pattern not only exists, but also enters your mind and *controls* your thinking and behavior. A pattern makes you *accountable* for something *not within your power, control or management.* It is a pattern that is *authoring* your problems. A pattern is the *cause,* and not you, although it cleverly presents you as the cause to the outside world as well as to yourself. It makes you *incapable of rational thoughts and actions* that are in your best interest.

This section describes what patterns do to your perceptions and thinking, where they come from, how they interact and how your lifestyle reinforces their operations.

What Patterns Do to Your Thinking

A pattern is to your memory of an unsettling event as electrical power is to a vending machine. A pattern's operation is similar to that of a vending machine for soda or candy; like a vending machine, a pattern cannot think and has no awareness of how much is enough. A pattern has only one purpose: its survival. When you encounter a situation, person, place or event that is even remotely similar to one that caused you the *original* upsetting feeling, your unconscious association with the historical event will cause you to feel the same upsetting feeling. The pattern, which is attached to the original memory, feeds on your upsetting emotions. Every situation is unique, but your emotions associated with the memory will cause you to react in a predictable way – a way that is usually painful for you, but nurturing for the pattern. The pattern keeps you from seeing what is really going on and prevents you from seeing other options and choices. Instead of effective responses, patterns cause you to *react,* which leads to endless "coulda, woulda, shoulda, oughta" instant replays in your mind and commiserating conversations.

By destroying the patterns within you, you effortlessly become aware of options and choices that support your being more balanced and present in the moment. Until you destroy the patterns, they will punitively slam the door in the face of your hopes and dreams leaving you feeling lost. Patterns use your rationalizations to intensify your feelings of desperation that you are irreparably flawed, that you deserve all your pain and suffering, and that you must have brought it upon yourself. You unwittingly become convinced that you are your worst enemy and the saboteur of your health and cherished dreams. You feel guilty and even stupid for not being able analyze and heal yourself after reading many self-help and new-age books. Many of these books blame you and hammer you into believing that and you alone, *somehow* are the creator of your failed relationships, social awkwardness, poor parenting, body tensions, heart attacks, chronic illnesses, addictions, depressions, as well as academic, athletic or employment disappointments.

David Found His Brother's Spirit All Better

David was a 30-year-old Native American whose physician had hospitalized him for numerous physical complaints. Extensive medical tests did not find any pathology, so he was released. His doctor believed David's symptoms were stress-related from the death of his grandmother compounded by the recent suicide of his younger 18-year-old brother, Benjamin. His physician delayed prescribing medications to treat David's anxiety and depression until I evaluated him.

Our initial session focused on David's enormous guilt over Benjamin's suicide. He said he would never forgive himself for not being more involved with his younger brother. Benjamin left high school because he had many problems, the biggest of which was his sexuality and people's response to it. David said, "Homosexuality in my brother's community was treated worse than having leprosy." He went on to say, "They crucified him with judgmental darts from their eyes and their hypocritical, hateful words from their sick hearts." David's guilt for a moment became secondary to his underlying anger and rage at the tragic suicide.

David's primary medical complaint was waking up daily with a tight and painful stomach. I told David to ask his imagination to pretend that a thing, person, situation, monster, etc. was making his stomach tight and painful. He said that it was a tied-up, twisted washcloth. I then had David ask the twisted washcloth what its intention was in generating his stomach problem. The image's first response was, "Fear". A second question he asked the image was, "How does it benefit you to do this to me?" The image replied, "It keeps me alive."

David had a parasitical pattern that maintained its existence at the expense of its host, in this case, David. I told him, "You don't want anything in your mind that sucks out your life force and generates your physical discomfort."

The next step for David was to imagine destroying the symbolic image of the tied-up washcloth. The washcloth appeared to resist his attempts to destroy it, so I offered him an idea: "Pretend that the washcloth is made of the same material as dried old newspapers, the ones you'd find in an attic." David said, "It's burned to ashes now." In its place he requested his imagination for an image to reconnect him to his spirit of calmness that was there long before he ever had the pain in his stomach. David commented, "It's the countryside where I grew up. I have always felt good there, but it feels tainted since my brother died. Whenever I think of Benjamin, I feel a profound loss." I instructed him to ask his imagination for it to come up with an image that just generated that feeling of "profound loss."

David said, "It's an image of an atom... and now it's becoming the black hole in outer space." When the black hole was asked its intention in creating the profound loss, it immediately responded, "To remind you it's the spirit of your brother, and it's supposed to make you feel it." David said he felt he was being pulled into the black hole, and he let it happen. The room we occupied was full of silence. Then tears were in his eyes.

After a while, I asked how he was doing and what he had experienced. With a warm smile, he said, "From inside the black hole looking out everything is all light. My brother is OK. His spirit told me so. It's all OK now, as I know where I can find him. After he died, I didn't know where his spirit was. But it's OK now. Whenever I want to be with Benjamin's spirit, I can go inside the hole and feel comforted." He described himself and his stomach as being very calm. He was told to welcome that positive image into his heart, spirit and every cell in his body like a sponge absorbing water.

The graphic image of the black hole gave David a powerful experience, one much greater than any insight he would have gotten from an intellectual discussion or explanation. Upon the annihilation of the tied-up wash cloth, the spontaneous image of the black hole provided a missing piece that destroyed the shackles of a pattern of unforgiving. In a follow-up call two weeks later, David's physician reaffirmed that David's pain symptoms completely abated.

How many of you are caught up in being righteously unforgiving of yourself or others? Always remember it is not you being unforgiving, but rather it is being orchestrated by an invisible pattern. Whenever you find yourself blaming yourself when things in life do not make any sense, you may want to think twice instead. First of all, forgive yourself with a compassionate full pardon. Then investigate the invisible world, the hiding place and residence of patterns within your unconscious mind. After you have done so, you can evaluate its worth for you. We believe you will find that unconditional self-love and self-compassion will no longer be words on a page in a book. Compassion and self-love will be the way you perceive yourself and others.

When the pattern makes it *appear* to you and others that you are not taking responsibility for what you are doing in your life, you need to notice how that false belief manifests in your life. You need to suspend for a moment what you believe is "reality" and be open to the possibility that there is an invisible "force" generating your *apparent* lack of responsibility. For example, a pattern plunges you into feelings of sadness, hopelessness, helplessness and unworthiness that can make you act "lazy" in the eyes of others. But the "lazy" behavior is totally orchestrated by the conniving, invisible pattern that runs its illusionary show from behind the scenes, out of your awareness. For example, when your child is acting lazy all the time, and you believe it is a phase he or she is going through and will outgrow in time, think twice. If medical causes have been ruled out, then chronic laziness is a red flag that a pattern is operating, which will manifest into a theme throughout your child's life like a low-grade depression or unhappiness until the pattern is destroyed.

Have the patterns twisted your sense of responsibility in order to ensure the patterns' own survival? Has the belief of your being responsible in creating everything in your life gone too far? Are the advocates of total responsibility too close to the trees to see the forest full of patterns that are hiding in plain view? Have total-responsibility proponents lost empathy and compassion for the people who blindly buy into it? Has the belief of total responsibility taken power over the masses? Has it unwittingly gone from its original intent of promoting empowerment and perseverance for self-healing into a boomerang of guilt, blame and shame? And even if you do not hold such punitive beliefs openly, do they still prowl somewhere in the back-room shadows of your inner thoughts?

Here is an example of how a pattern attaches itself to a memory: A person who as a child was frightened by a clown wearing a yellow outfit, years late will feel uncomfortable, anxious and scared simply by seeing a photo of a clown, a clown on TV or a clown at children's party or circus - or even seeing any adult wearing yellow. The person is focused on the feeling and does not even suspect that a pattern is operating on the memory within him or her. Everyone has a set of aversions to certain foods, clothing, colors, aromas, animals, etc. from earlier in their lives that are triggered by patterns as adults. This is just how common patterns are in all of us.

This does not imply that all automatic reactions are bad. We all go through our daily lives in an automatic mode. That is, much of our daily activities is done at the unconscious level - from eating our meals to driving our cars to carrying on our conversations - we rely a great deal on our unconscious programming.

This automatic programming is necessary in order to carry on our lives efficiently. If it were not for unconscious programming, every activity necessary for our daily lives would require a formidable set of deliberate, conscious decisions. The need to think about every step involved in the simplest of activities would be exhausting, and the pace of our lives, hectic as it may be, would become unimaginably slow. Emergencies would be averted, while others would proceed beyond containment. And so our automatic programming mode is definitely a great asset.

Yes, you may brush your teeth and put on your coat in an automatic mode, but almost everything else you do is pre-programmed as well - even your inner thoughts! It is the pattern that filters the energy and shapes it into a thought that is compatible with the pattern's energy. The emotion that results from that thought is one that feeds and reinforces the pattern. This process is illustrated in the following diagram:

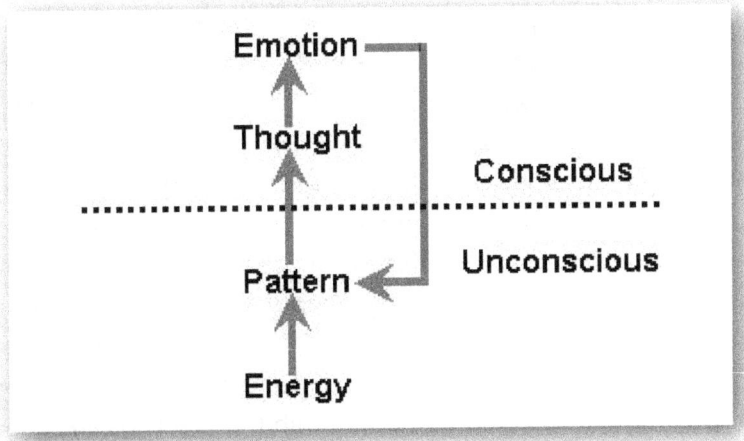

Events are neutral; your emotional reaction is programmed. If experience came with an attached emotion, attitude or reaction, then the same experience would have an identical effect on everyone.

But nothing that you experience has an attached emotion, meaning or feeling. If your experience contained an attached emotion, or meaning or feeling, then changing your mood would be simply a matter of reading or listening to words that contain the desired emotion. A single word, completely out of context, can produce different emotions in different people. The sound of children's laughter can produce happiness in one person and sadness in another. So if different people experience different emotions in response to the same situation, then obviously the situation itself is neutral, without any attached emotion, meaning or feeling. Something inside you – a pattern – controls how you perceive, think and react.

A pattern will prevent you from seeing anything that threatens its existence. A pattern will permit you to see only that option that is in the best interests of the pattern, namely its survival. A pattern's survival depends upon your automatic, upsetting emotions, such as anger or sadness that results from a pattern's dictating your behavior. Annihilating a pattern ends all the associated upsetting emotions that made you identify with a story of your "false self." The death of a pattern allows you to live with greater inner peace and joy.

But, for many people, the mere consideration of destroying a malicious pattern produces great discomfort. Many people would literally rather die than even *consider* giving up a harmful pattern, even if that pattern causes them great misery. This is because the pattern convinces them that if the pattern is destroyed, then they will be destroyed or disappear along with it. The pattern has convinced them that the pattern and they are one. Cigarettes, coffee, alcohol and texting are common examples of patterns' control that many people wrestle with. In most cases, the pattern has been with them throughout their lives, and they have no vision of what their lives would be without the feelings that the pattern produces. People have come to identify with their feelings and even give them labels – victim, addict, rescuer, defender, people pleaser, righteous protector, martyr, failure, procrastinator, always late, etc. For most people, the set of patterns within them is their self-image that controls how they will predictably behave in a given situation.

This does not mean that only specific situations, and no others are subject to a pattern's operations, because a pattern affects all areas of your life. A consistent set of unrewarding relationships may also affect your ability to find success with some other activity. The pattern that causes your frustrating relationships at home or work may also be operating on your inconsistent golf game. In this example, the seemingly unrelated problems at home, at work and on the golf course are caused by the same pattern of frustration.

Like termites feed on the foundation of a home, patterns feed on upsetting emotions, because patterns form under traumatic, frightening, anxiety-provoking, threatening, etc. circumstances. The emotions that you felt when the pattern originally began its operation are the ones that it uses to maintain and reinforce itself. Consider a child who, while playing with her toys, is praised, hugged or kissed by her parent. Now consider the same child who, while playing with her toys, is yelled at, threatened or beaten by her parent. Which scenario will produce a pattern that will cause her to have lifetime feelings of worry, low self-esteem, fear or mistrust? A pattern's operations can readily be detected in your life when you realize that you are encountering a situation that has consistently repeated itself throughout your life.

A pattern in you, and not you, will attract patterns in others that will ignite emotions that will feed the patterns' energy needs in you and others. Your reactions to life's situations affect everyone around you. Others' behaviors toward you are influenced on both the conscious and unconscious levels by their perceptions of where your 'hot buttons' are located. Others will use certain words, phrases and body language to control your reactions. For example, a lukewarm response to your joyful news may cause you to question your initial joyous emotion.

Together Again All Better
I worked with Charlie a number of years ago and he claimed it changed his life. Over the past couple of years Charlie had become increasingly worried about his 27-year-old son, Chris. There was no longer any meaningful communication between them as tension had formed a chasm and nothing Charlie did or suggested could bridge it. He was at his wit's end, yet was able to convince Chris to drive with him to my office for a session.

Chris had several issues he wanted to address: 1) "I'm disappointed with myself in the relationship with my dad because he's disappointed with me. I have a depressed feeling in my body regarding the poor relationship with him." 2) "People take advantage of me because I'm too trusting." And 3) "I have resentment about how I present myself to others, how I come across to them." I had him call upon his imagination to present him images that were associated with these issues. Images that represented the patterns were annihilated. His imagination was then able to present him with positive images that represented his desired outcome of feeling calm, safe and confident.

The biggest shift that took place upon lighting up his central pathway was when Chris' face transformed into a pink healthy color and a warm endearing smile appeared, much like an innocence you see on a child's face. I asked if he was aware of that feeling in his face and a big smile I had not seen before. Chris said, "Yes. My face feels warm all over. I feel happy." He was unable to feel any of the upsetting emotions associated with the any of those issues we addressed as a number of patterns had been destroyed.

His father called me a few days later and said, "Thank you for giving me my son back. I thought I had lost him. He was whistling in the car on our way back home from seeing you. He hasn't whistled in over a year. And his supervisor at my plant where Chris works asked, 'What happened to Chris? He's a different person. Upbeat. Positive. The difference is like night and day!'"

Chris' description was, "I'm in control of my own destiny now." He gave an example of how he appropriately confronted a so-called friend who had taken advantage of him and owed him money. Chris no longer took what his dad said personally and he found himself having positive choices that came to mind while interacting with his father.

Imagine All Better offers you freedom.

6

How a Pattern Defends Itself

*"Thought and analysis are powerless to pierce the great
mystery that hovers over the world and
over our existence."*

— Dr. Albert Schweitzer

A PATTERN IS YOUR invisible opponent that feeds on your upsetting emotional energies. It modifies your perceptions to cause you to generate upsetting emotions about processes, events and behaviors. Until you become aware of a pattern and its operations, the pattern will continue to grow and become stronger in your life. A pattern also uses your upsetting emotional energy to defend itself. When your awareness approaches a pattern's existence, the pattern causes you to generate upsetting, unpleasant emotions and feelings. Remembering or imagining the associated scenario is an unpleasant experience.

The pattern thus defends itself from your awareness by causing you to "do something" about the effects of its operation. Of course, doing something will always fail because the pattern can never be satisfied. Its demands for your upsetting emotional energy cannot and will never be satisfied. Its operation is similar to that of a vending machine: like a vending machine, a pattern cannot think and has no awareness of how much is enough. A pattern has only one purpose: its survival. A pattern is to our memory of an event as electrical power is to a vending machine. A pattern powers your automatic perspective, upsetting emotions and behavior.

A pattern within you is a bit of organized energy that vibrates. Everything, including thoughts, is made of energy and all energy vibrates at a given frequency. A pattern, like a magnet, attracts those memories, images, feelings and behaviors that vibrate at a sympathetic, or resonant, frequency of the pattern in you and in others. A pattern therefore has no need to think, since it instantly and automatically attracts to itself every bit of your personal information that it needs to defend itself. And it makes use of the entire contents of your unconscious – everything that has ever happened to you together with your entire genetic heritage! Whenever you encounter a situation that has the tiniest bit of similarity to an upsetting feeling from your past, a pattern will use the complex web that it has assembled to make you feel an unwanted feeling. And since you believe that what you are feeling is as 'real' as you are, you automatically assume that the pattern and your feelings are who you are.

In fact, you are not your patterns or the feelings that their operations generate within you. Patterns that do not serve you are energetic parasites that rely on your upsetting emotions of worry, anger, despair, etc. for their continued existence. Until a pattern is destroyed it will continue to structure your life and cause you to experience a repeating, familiar sequence of circumstances. So, if you find yourself asking, "How did I get myself into this situation – again?" "How do I always find losers?" begin to look for your patterns. It is your patterns, not you, who got you there – again and again. As long as you remain focused on your upsetting feelings and continue to analyze those feelings, the pattern remains hidden behind an ever-growing defensive wall of feelings that you do not want. Personal and collective histories thus repeat themselves endlessly because patterns are never discovered and destroyed.

In summary, a pattern defends itself by getting you to believe that you are the pattern, that you sabotage your life and you are your worst enemy. That is, you identify so closely with its operation that you never question whether or not your reaction to a given situation is proper or effective. Your lack of awareness prevents you from seeing the operation of the pattern and blocks your ability to see other options that are proper in the moment. You react automatically and predictably in response to a pattern that you identify with as 'me'. It is like being in a trance, drugged or under a spell. You see others' patterns operating, but rarely your own. You are forever giving good advice to your children, spouses, parents, significant others, clients and friends, but not to yourself. Or if you do, then that advice evaporates before you ever fully implement it.

Imagine All Better offers you freedom.

7

Patterns Determine How You Interpret and React to Situations

"The only way out is in."

— SHELDON KOPP

WHENEVER YOU ENCOUNTER a situation that is even remotely similar to a memory that triggers a pattern onto action, you have the emotion or feeling associated with the *original* memory and you assign a meaning to the *current* experience. The process takes place spontaneously in the right brain where your unconscious resides. You are unaware that the pattern's action is taking place, and you assume that the reaction is yours and is normal, acceptable and justified. If you examine your reaction, you will always find that you can rationalize your behavior and emotions because the pattern will permit you to see only those options that do not threaten its existence. These rationales are the patterns' colored lenses through which you view the world. This manipulation by patterns has been going on since time began, and you never knew it – until now! If you examine your behavior without looking through those patterns' colored lenses, with an unadulterated perception, then you will see what is really going on, and respond effectively, rather than react, to every situation.

However, until you destroy it, a pattern will cause you to react and behave in a way that feeds its energy requirements, which consist of the energy in upsetting emotions. Because a pattern will always motivate you to meet its energy needs and ensure its continued existence, anything that you do that is motivated by a pattern will strengthen the pattern. Typical coping strategies for dealing with patterns include avoiding unpleasant thoughts or situations, reciting affirmations that counteract the unpleasant emotions or situations, and verbally repeating your story.

You perceive and give meaning to the world or what you call 'reality' through the eyes, ears and feelings projected onto it by a pattern. You generally become aware of a pattern's existence and operation through emotionally draining situations. Examples are an illness or the recognition of a repeating undesirable result, such as an outstanding baseball player's demotion because he spiraled into a slump at the plate that neither he nor his coaches could resolve. Another example is getting bad grades despite hours of study. These frustrating situations in no way imply that you are personally responsible for consciously intending your illness, disappointment or undesirable result.

Alex played professional baseball for several years until a repeating pattern made him struggle mightily whenever hitting. He was brilliant at everything else in baseball, except at the plate, which eventually led to his release. He loved baseball so he became a coach until one day a pattern was awakened while pitching to young players. Fear took over. Alex could not get the thoughts out of his mind of hitting a player on the head with the ball. Then it happened. But the player wore a helmet that protected him, and he was OK. However, Alex was not. We worked together and addressed the patterns of fear, anxiety and What-If dialogs in his head until he felt completely confident throwing the ball. His doubts never returned.

As many writers have shown, we are not a body and a mind that are separated by some distinct boundary, but rather we are a bodymind with no clear boundaries. The patterns that go undetected in your mind affect your body and the outcomes that you perceive. Medical science is aware that depression and sadness have a detrimental effect on the body's immune system and render you more likely to become ill. By removing the associated emotional content of your medical symptoms, such as fear and anxiety, Imagine All Better restores your balance, calms your mind and thus enhances and promotes your bodymind's healing capabilities.

During an annual physical a year ago, Frieda's doctor discovered her immune system was seriously compromised. He was baffled why a physically fit young lady on a sports scholarship could have it in the first place and function so well. Upon hearing her diagnosis, Frieda became so fearful that she imagined the worst scenarios. During the past couple of years, she had lost her favorite grandfather due to cancer and experienced the deaths of a cousin, an aunt and surviving grandparents. The recent bitter divorce between her parents was yet another huge loss. She felt that the foundation of her 'reality' was collapsing all around her.

Once we worked on the patterns of depression, sadness and fear, and she destroyed them, her calmness and confidence returned. She handled her parent's divorce much better and her medical tests showed that her immune system dramatically returned to normal.

Queen of Picking and Choosing My Battles All Better

All concerned benefit when a pattern is destroyed. My initial session with Kathy was lengthy, over an hour and a half. Kathy believed she had nothing in particular to address. She knew she had stress in her life and believed she was coping with it as best as anyone could. She believed the situations causing the stress were real and she had to "grin and bear it."

I initially addressed Kathy's frustration of being stressed that she rated as an eight on a zero-to-10 scale. I remotely lit up her central pathway with gold light numerous times as she focused on a particularly stressful memory. Within a couple of minutes, it was a zero. The next emotion she worked on was associated with a situation that made her angry. She rated it a nine. I lit up her central pathway several more times and Kathy reported the intensity of her anger going down to a three. I continued lighting up her central pathway and when I asked for the number she said, "It's not important any more. It's gone. I can't find it."

Then she commented, "If it happens again, I can handle it as I've perfected picking and choosing my battles." Whenever she avoided a confrontation, Kathy would grit her teeth until her jaw hurt. I asked her to give me some examples of angry situations in which she avoids confrontations and grits her teeth. She mentioned her frustration occurs when certain people are complaining. Kathy said, "I hate when people are complaining." I asked who the complaining people were that come to mind. She listed her husband, four children and her mother. Oh, then she added her ex-husband!

I started to work with the image of her mother followed by that of her ex-husband. My intuition was that by working with the images of these two people, she would resolve the anger she experienced with her husband and children. I had Kathy focus on these specific persons who made her angry as opposed to asking her imagination to give her an image that made her angry.

"Kathy, get an image of your mother in your mind's eye that is associated with intense anger. Quietly in your mind so I don't hear it, look at her image and only tell her how you feel. Don't blame her. Only educate her image how you feel whenever she behaves in ways that trigger irritation and annoyance - ways that make you usually keep your mouth shut. Tell her what you experienced emotionally, physically, or physiologically during those moments. Only tell her what you feel and nothing else. For example, tell her, "I feel annoyed;" "I feel dismissed;" "I feel tension in my stomach, etc." Educate her as if you're a teacher educating a five-year-old for the first time."

"I did so and my mother is crying."

"Remind her that you are not blaming her, but rather expressing what you feel inside that you have never shared before."

"Now she smiles."

"I would take that as a positive response (little did I know I was wrong). Since the mother's image appears to be positive about what you said, tell her to transform herself into the most positive image with the most positive energy that can reconnect you to feel unconditional self-acknowledgment and unconditional self-acceptance."

"The image starts crying again, uncontrollably crying."

Her mother's image responded by making it all about herself, not Kathy. Since her mother's image went on and on and on, and did not acknowledge Kathy's request, I told Kathy to destroy it. Images in the imagination are symbolic, so you are not harming a person by destroying their image. You are telling your imagination that you no longer want that image that doesn't acknowledge you.

"Pretend the image of your mother is a photograph or piece of film and either put a match to it, shred it or cut it into pieces…whatever comes to mind."

"Did it."

"Now ask your imagination for it, and not you, to come up with the most positive image with the most positive energy that can reconnect you to your original spirit of unconditional love, unconditional self-acceptance and unconditional acknowledgment."

"It's my grandmother."

"Ask your grandmother if she is here to help do all that and more for you."

"She hugs me."

"Now welcome the image of your grandmother to come inside you."

"Now see if there's any doubt or skepticism either in a feeling in your body, an emotional feeling or some thoughts or voice in your head talking you out of that image being able to help."

"None. I feel very good with my grandma."

"You mentioned your ex-husband is also associated with this anger."

"That's where I learned to grit my teeth. He was highly emotional and explosive in our house."

"Conjure up an image of him in one of those angry moods. Now ask him, 'What do you personally get from making me grit my teeth?'"

"It's an image of his having a tantrum and stomping his feet. He's very scary."

"No need to ask any more questions than that. Destroy his symbolic image. It's a pattern called an 'Attitude'.

"I have him totally nude standing in front of the congregation he leads as a minister. I want him to squirm and feel embarrassed."

"Enjoy it as long as you want, but in time your imagination would need to have you create his image as being annihilated so we can move onto the next step of getting you to feel the way you've wanted to feel for many years. You could imagine him as a statue or a fragile glass figurine and have a boulder fall from the sky and smash him. Or anything else that comes to mind."

"Did it. He's in pieces all over the ground."

"How would you like to feel?"

She thought for a moment and relied, "Open."

"Now tell your imagination to welcome back the most positive image with the most positive energy that can reconnect you to your spirit of feeling open."

"It's a butterfly and it's flying around to and fro. Now it's flying toward me and just landed on my finger. I'm OK now that it's landed on my finger. I already felt like it was partnering with me regarding whatever 'open' is, and that we would find it. The butterfly is now rubbing its front feet together as it rests on my finger."

"Well done. Welcome the butterfly to come inside your heart, spirit and every cell in your body."

I contacted Kathy 10 days later to learn that her perceptions had shifted. I was delighted in what I heard.

"I didn't know I was doing badly before, but now I feel different. Before I saw you, I didn't feel like I had a problem. I knew there was stress with others in the family and at work, but it didn't make me sick, neurotic, take drugs, drink or have erratic behaviors. I was handling it well, but in hindsight, I was only handling half of it. It has been very freeing and opening not to hold onto that other half of it any more.

I feel like I have a little thing to trick my brain and no longer have to hold onto things or feelings and put them off until later, or never at all like I've always done. My current husband, Charlie, remarked that instead of letting things go like I had been doing, I was now discussing things with him that I wouldn't normally do, and in a nice manner. He said in the past that I would never "challenge" him on issues.

Last Saturday, as I sat down at the dining room table to have dinner, I became transfixed on a painting hanging on the wall, which has been there for many years. My girlfriend from high school some 40 years ago painted it as a gift. It's a little girl with a butterfly on her finger. I stared at it during most of the dinner. It gave me, not chills, but a feeling of being amazed. I didn't connect with it until Saturday night!"

"What about the issues gritting your teeth tightly until your jaw hurt?"

"That's a thing of the past. My husband asked me, 'How's it going? Have you been using that new technique?' I didn't have to do anything, as nothing upset me like it used to. I was no longer holding onto any upsets. I was spontaneously speaking up. It happened so naturally. It took me by surprise! It's been a very enlightening couple of weeks.

Charlie asked if I were aware of any changes since you and I worked together. First of all, I no longer walk out of a room when he introduces certain conversations. In the past, I would have gritted my teeth. But now I am standing up for myself, not only at home, but also at work. I work 20 hours a week and have always complied with everyone's request. I would do whatever I was asked, which would result in my taking work home and not being paid for it, as I could not do all the work during the 20 hours. I was working on weekends for no money. Now what I find myself doing automatically is asking the person or my supervisor who asks me to do additional work, 'What do you want to trade for the extra work?' I was surprised how everybody came up with a trade-off that worked for me. I thought to myself, 'Why didn't I do that years ago?' I am no longer Queen of Pick and Choose Your Battles."

"Since that false identity is no longer you, how do you see your new identity?"

"After our session together I did a lot of thinking driving home: 'If I'm not this person who holds onto emotions, what emotions are left? Who am I? And if I am no longer a people-pleaser, who am I?' And then an answer came to me without thinking: 'I am Kathy-Pleaser.' I would always feel selfish putting myself first. But now I have a right to be happy and determine what I want and what I need. I have that right again."

"Good for you. I remember many years ago when a mother would have her young child sitting next to her on an airplane. The cabin attendant would remind the passengers that in case of an emergency, oxygen masks from above would fall down, and if they were traveling with any children to put the mask on their own face at first and secure it. Then put the oxygen mask on their child's face and secure it. Most mothers were freaked out over hearing such blasphemy. Their belief was: 'I am always last. My child comes first.' However, if the mother doesn't put the oxygen mask on her face first, she may not have the strength to place the oxygen mask on her child's face. Mothers need to nourish and nurture themselves in order to provide the best care for their children. So there is nothing wrong with being a self-pleaser, Kathy-pleaser. By taking care of yourself first, you have the energy and where-with-all to then handle others' needs."

Kathy continued her story. It got even better. "The butterfly keeps bubbling up without my thinking about it. It presents itself as a thought in my brain - and the butterfly flies into my brain. I don't know how else to explain it. Somehow the butterfly has allowed me to be open without any mental rehearsing or conversations inside my head, of 'He'll say, I'll say, he'll say, I'll say'. None of that is present. I'm just open to say what needs to be said *without thinking*.

I'll give you an example. Charlie likes grapes - a lot. When I come home from work, I find grape stems on the kitchen counter, on the bar, on the bathroom sinks. Everywhere. Charlie sees me picking up the grape stems now with no attitude about it. I just pick them up. Previously my thoughts were to be upset while doing so. The wildest thing has happened. Charlie, without a word from me, has stopped leaving grape stems around. I have no idea how that happened. Something raised his consciousness. Charlie's more aware. And I have no frustration picking them up. There is no emotion attached to it anymore.

During the past two weeks, I've started writing a little. I haven't written in a long time. I wrote about the butterfly and a bicycle image that came to me, kind of like how the butterfly image did on its own. The one about the bicycle had to do with times in my life I had been out of control, and now I'm in control. I'm riding the bike, and I have choices to do what I want to do; take a left or right or continue straight ahead. On the bicycle, I'm in control. And I don't have to pick up anyone on my ride. It's very freeing. It's a great metaphor for the transformation that has taken place.

Another example is my normal routine on Fridays when I came home from work was to bring work home. This past Friday, instead of logging in, I sat down and wrote these two stories. Then I googled 'art work,' and spent an hour and a half of not being productive. It was strange not to be working. Now I have a way to deal with all this. I call it a trick; like a magic trick and positive experiences continue to appear from the middle of nowhere."

Imagine All Better offers you freedom.

8

Patterns and Thought Clutter

*"Greed is so well organized that we call it economic prosperity.
Ill will is so well organized that we call it defense and we make weapons and war.
Ignorance is so well organized that we study about everything except ourselves.
I try to decrease the thoughts in my mind.
If we stopped thinking we'd have no problems."*

— A.T. Ariyaratne, the Gandhi of Sri Lanka

As you destroy more patterns, the number and volume of the voices in your internal chatter will diminish, and peace becomes your normal internal state. When there are no patterns to shape your thoughts, which are distortions of the pure energy field from which a thought is formed, then what remains is the quiet of the energy source itself. Your natural state is one of peace, and not the worry, anxiety, or sadness that previously fed the pattern that caused those upsetting emotions and their constant background chatter.

Your ongoing chatter takes no time off, and you try to mask it when you use alcohol, prescription and recreational drugs or cigarettes, eat until the bag of cookies or chips is emptied, listen to your personal MP3 players, talk on your cell phones, text message or play video games. The popular theories about the racing thoughts include reactions to stress, poor diet and a succession of unsolved personal problems that characterize your life. However, these hypothetical reasons are not causes of the inner chatter, but are the *effects* of patterns at work. Patterns are the cause of your ongoing chatter, inner conflict and inability to know what is really happening right now, in this unique moment.

Your pattern-free decisions will be based on what is happening in the moment. The decision will come from your right-brain wisdom rather than your left-brain logic. Consider going to a restaurant or buffet line and selecting a meal. How do you choose what you would like to eat? You make your selection based upon the appeal the description the food has, which does not involve the left brain, your intellectual analysis. In other words, you *'know without thinking'* what you would like to eat. Ordering it based on your cholesterol levels and the price of that two- pound lobster is another story!

You have many examples in your life in which you instinctively knew what to do and what the result would be if you acted on that instinct. Instead, you 'thought it over', analyzed every *apparent* option, discussed it with friends or coworkers and then went with your 'best' choice, not your 'gut feeling'. And surprise! Your instinct would have worked out best. How many times in cases like this have you ended up saying, "I told me so!"? Your instinct, your 'gut feeling', is what 'knowing without thinking' is all about. The patterns within you keep you second-guessing yourself, analyzing your feelings and diverting your attention from what is going on right in front of you. Patterns cannot be pacified or made into allies; patterns must be destroyed or they will destroy you.

As you destroy the patterns within you, you will know without thinking in the moment how to respond. Being free of patterns will not give you the knowledge that is necessary to sit for a certification examination or get a university degree without attending classes. However, being free of patterns will allow you to be more effective in understanding and applying your knowing without thinking. Being free of patterns will eliminate your inner chatter and "woulda, coulda, shoulda, oughta" discussions because you will know without thinking what the proper action is in the moment.

The following vignettes summarize our clients' minds returning to an inner peacefulness as the noise of constant chattering dissipated like air coming out of a balloon following Imagine All Better.

Janice is an executive with a national consulting firm. The patterns had her convinced that nothing that she could ever do would be enough to satisfy her clients and the senior management in her firm. She therefore felt compelled to work long hours, weekends and holidays and sacrifice her vacation time. She felt emotionally depleted and near the verge of quitting her job to preserve her health. I worked with her to destroy a set of patterns from her childhood that had repeated her drama throughout her career. A few weeks after our sessions, she called to report that: "For the first time in my life, I am able to meditate because my background chatter is almost gone." Up until then, the chatter was so loud that she found it impossible to experience the silence that meditation brings.

Lisa is an actress, a yoga instructor and a personal trainer. Over the years repeating patterns had generated a series of bad relationships and the end of her last breakup led her to call me. A couple of months after she had two sessions in which she annihilated the patterns causing these problems, she said: "I can confidently say now, life has definitely changed for the better. The cloudy, cluttered state of mind I carried with me has all but disappeared, giving way to a wonderful sense of calm and stillness. Problems don't loom so large, and the stillness inside me allows me space to step back and discern, unemotionally, how to deal with them."

Former Pittsburgh Pirates pitcher and broadcaster Steve Blass was a 19-game-winner in 1972. Shortly afterward Blass lost his strike zone, feared hitting batters and his career ended in 1975. Steve's well-publicized inexplicable throwing problems gave rise to label subsequent pitchers on the verge of losing their careers as having the "Steve Blass disease". After working with Blass at spring training in Florida for 90 minutes, he destroyed the pattern that had destroyed his baseball career and threw his first strike in a quarter of a century! I was thrilled to witness his transformation. It was like living a moment from the film *Field of Dreams*. In Blass' book, *A Pirate for Life*, he documents his incredible rise and painful fall from grace, and how in his sixties he successfully pitched 8 and 2/3 innings with the same mindset he had when he was at the top of his game in major league baseball.

Later, Blass wrote his perspective that appeared in my baseball book, *Mentalball*: "I had been approached by many well-intentioned people to help me overcome my control problems without success. Your approach was the only thing that worked. I'm firmly convinced that one of the biggest problems in such these cases as mine is that too many suggestions, ideas, theories, etc. can cause clutter. In my mind, clutter is the worst part of the problem. Your technique was able to help me completely remove the clutter that allowed me to return to the simplicity that is so critical to success. I wish I had met you in 1972 or '74. There is much to be said for early detection."

Imagine All Better offers you freedom.

9

Patterns and Stories

*"There is no reality except the one contained within us;
that is why so many people live such an unreal life.
They take the images outside them for reality and never
allow the world within to assert itself."*

— Herman Hesse, Recipient of the Nobel Prize in Literature

We are a species that makes extensive use of stories to bring order and a sense of continuity to our lives. Histories, myths, fairy tales and personal experiences are all connected by a story theme and supply our individual and collective needs to understand, explain, warn or justify situations and events. All cultures throughout all eras have used stories to pass acquired wisdom and knowledge to succeeding generations. However, patterns, and <u>not</u> you, organize *your* personal stories, that is, how you identify yourself and relate to others. The patterns manipulate and give meanings to the characters, plot lines and outcomes in your life.

Every witness to an automobile accident will have a different version of what happened. The patterns in every person will cause him or her to report the event differently. The patterns that form your stories keep you from seeing what is going on in the moment.

A story is a parable that represents a pattern and its activities, which reside in the right brain, the realm of your unconscious mind. A pattern that powers your personal story hides itself and its operation by convincing you that the emotion or perception it generates is who you are. A pattern performs its deception by operating in your unconscious, away from your conscious awareness. If a pattern is not destroyed, then the pattern causes you to believe the story that the pattern is attached to. That story becomes your false identity, and that story will repeat its plot line again and again in relationships, family interactions, employment, etc. You then accept without question the story's plot line as your life's theme, as your lot in life, as your fate. The pattern now dictates that you act out the story that it has written, and you unknowingly use to generate your upsetting emotions.

Reflect on how many popular entertainers over the years have destroyed their careers or their lives and that of their loved ones – or died from alcohol and drug abuse or suicide: Marilyn Monroe, Jim Morrison, Jimi Hendrix, Elvis Presley, Judy Garland, Whitney Houston, Heath Ledger, Philip Seymour Hoffman, Robin Williams, etc. That was the work of patterns manipulating them all along. And patterns would never allow them to follow their intuition, the positive advice of their agents, fans or loved ones to give up their destructive ways. The patterns made sure of that!

People within a culture acquire a set of personal stories from their families, authority figures and peers. Each of you also develops your own stories from your interpretations of significant life circumstances. While our collective histories, myths and fairy tales influence our perceptions, your individual, personalized stories go beyond perception itself: you live your stories. Your stories, organized by patterns, live through you while you remain unaware of their existences and operations.

Story statements, or beliefs, such as: "No matter what I do, it's never good enough.", "I always make bad choices.", "I have major character flaws.", "I can't complete anything I start.", "I never learn from my mistakes.", "I can't help it; it's just the way I am.", "I'm always tired; I have no energy.", "I never get a break." and "Why do I always find losers?" show a pattern's deception. These stories cause you to focus your attention on your thinking and the associated upsetting emotions that feed the pattern. When you reach a level of discomfort with some facet of your life – a relationship, job, boss, finances – you will begin to look for relief in your inner world through religion, meditation, spiritual practices or therapy. Each of these inner-directed approaches focuses on some element or elements of your turmoil such as a person, event or activity from your past or present, all of which are completely neutral. No story element has an emotion, meaning or purpose attached to it independent of your perception – or more correctly, the perception organized by a pattern operating within you.

Your story, your ego, your self-image is neither good nor bad, neither right nor wrong. Your story is the commandeered perception of 'reality', filtered through the upsetting emotions engineered by the patterns, that changes the interpretation of the same story from person to person. Since the stories' details are themselves emotionally neutral, a pattern organizes the emotional energy that the pattern attaches to your stories. A pattern triggers your predictable or customary behavior, such as being embarrassed by your parents' stories of you as a child. That pattern uses your emotional energy of embarrassment to survive and reinforce itself. Your parents have patterns in them that cause them to press your button of embarrassment in front of your friends. When either the pattern in you or the ones in your parents are destroyed, that upsetting emotion ends for good.

Each of your personal life stories has a unique element, such as specific individuals, places and times. But there is a limited number of themes that form the dominant, emotional tone of each of your stories that you tell yourself and others. The finite number of themes allows you to empathize with each other's stories and, if you are not careful, reinforce the pattern behind the stories by agreeing with, and supporting, the storyteller's version of what happened, such as, "You're right. Men are all bastards!" Since the stories' details are themselves emotionally neutral, a pattern is behind the emotional energy that you unconsciously attach to your stories. A pattern uses your and others' emotional energy to survive and reinforce itself. Destroying a pattern leaves you with only the memory of your story's details, but with no remaining emotional attachment to the story itself. Imagine what a relief that can be in your life!

Some common illustrations of story themes are worry, anger, confusion, grief, regret, shame, blame, disappointment, rejection, loneliness, hopelessness and despair. For example, "When I was in the sixth-grade play, and I forgot my lines, everybody laughed at me and since then I have always dreaded speaking in public. I've avoided jobs where I would have to make presentations." and, "Dad told me when I was struggling with my homework in the fifth grade that I was stupid and broccoli had a higher IQ than me, and that I would be better off marrying rich or joining the Army when I grow up."

Laura's Fear of Flying All Better
While flying from Indianapolis to Los Angeles and then on to Albuquerque on my way to Taos, New Mexico, I sat next to Laura, a 16-year-old girl who had the window seat. Two young children sitting directly behind us were squealing with delight as they took turns looking and pointing out the window. However, the passenger sitting next to me never once glanced out the window. She kept rigidly looking straight ahead. I then noticed she had a death grip on her plastic, lunchbox-styled purse. After we received our food, I engaged her in conversation and learned: "This is the first and last flight of my life! My father made me fly. I didn't want to do it, ever! I wanted to visit my grandparents who are very old

and may not be around much longer. But I wanted to drive across country. Not fly."

"Since you've never flown, how did you arrive at the decision that you never ever wanted to do so?"

"Because planes are scary. I'd feel a whole lot safer behind the wheel of a car. But, oh no. My father won't let me drive. So he made me fly this stupid thing."

After describing my qualifications, I shared with Laura that, "I've been working on an approach to help relieve tension and fear, and maybe it can help you right now. It doesn't take much time, and it all takes place in your imagination. Would you want to see what your reaction to it is?" I was surprisingly greeted with a whole-hearted, "Yes!"

"Good. Then pretend that this scary feeling that has you afraid of flying on planes, especially this one, is no longer a feeling but rather an image you can see. Quietly in your mind, tell your imagination, and not you, to give you an image, cartoon, monster, person, situation, object, character that makes you afraid to fly on an airplane. Let me know whatever comes to mind."

"It's Lestat. You know, the vampire from Anne Rice's book."

I then walked her through the process and Lestat only responded with sinister attitudes that upset her. So it wasn't difficult for her to destroy him. She pondered as to what experience she now wanted back with her since the symbol of his evil fear was gone. Finally, she decided she wanted to be re-connected with her own sense of feeling "free" and "protected." She then imagined an angel and described herself as feeling very relaxed. There was silence for several minutes.

Out of the corner of my eye, I noticed she had released her hands from her purse and was looking out the window for the first time.

"How are you doing now?"

"Huh?" she said. "Oh, I was just thinking how wonderful it is flying in the middle of the sky. I am overwhelmed by its beauty."

"Are you aware of being any more relaxed?"

"Unbelievably so!"

We encountered some turbulence and she started to grab the arm rests, then released them quickly saying with a smile: "These bumps are no worse than the ones my grandparents find when driving. They managed to hit every pot hole in the road."

She was already seeing the same situation very differently now. As we approached landing, her anxiety initiated another conversation with me about what to expect when the plane touched ground. I explained, "Landing could be anywhere on a continuum of very smooth to a sharp jolt. Yet, you get to applaud the pilots when we land if you wish." Upon landing she commented, "That wasn't so bad after all."

She no longer was viewing flying through the lens of fear. I told her, "Now that you have such a different attitude about flying, maybe you'll eventually become a flight attendant and one day we would meet again in the air." Laura smiled and said, "If I ever do, I'll make sure you have a window seat in first class." She proceeded to give me a high-five.

Anxiety All Better

When I continued on my connecting flight to Albuquerque, I had the opportunity of sitting next to Dr. Paul Zarutskie, an invitro fertilization pioneer. I felt like I was turning into the Johnny Appleseed of the airlines planting seeds of relaxation using Imagine All Better. While the imagination process we did together made no logical sense to Paul's mind, he was amazed that he could resolve his extreme anxiety about being an expert witness the next morning "simply by moving images around in my mind." The entire process took less than ten minutes.

I asked Paul, "How do you know it will be effective when you are in court tomorrow?" He said, "Because I felt a wave of warm, tingling relaxation feeling take over my entire body when that positive image came inside me. I then imagined myself being in the courtroom tomorrow and saw myself at peace and as confident as I am performing surgery." Paul contacted me when he returned to California to report that the positive results continued and invited me to teach the technique to his staff, meet his family and be their houseguest in Laguna Niguel. Not a bad exchange for ten minutes of my time.

Imagine All Better offers you freedom.

10

Intellect and Imagination

"Mysteries are not to be solved.
The eye goes blind
When it only wants to see why."

— Rumi, 13th-century Persian poet

We live in an age in which we believe that the scientific method will find the answers to just about every problem that we have, from global warming and disease to conflict resolution and psychological torment. Our culture encourages and rewards intellectual development and there is much to be said for intellectual development. Because of logical investigation, we have aircraft, satellites, antibiotics, automobiles, microelectronics, the Internet, and instant communications. Our knowledge is doubling at an exponential rate. It would appear that all of our problems could be solved if we could only analyze them and develop enough knowledge. But studying and talking about the "tracks" left by a pattern in our conscious perception is not the same as finding the cunning pattern that makes those tracks from its hiding place in the unconscious. The pattern causes us to mistake the symptoms *it* causes for the cause itself, and then to embrace and defend the mistake.

Once something is learned, the pattern in the discoverer causes the discoverer to defend the discovery. Any discovery that is challenged with conflicting information triggers a defensive pattern. Once a body of knowledge is widely accepted, it tends to become dogma for the individuals who have based their training, practices, careers, certifications and analysis methods upon it. Conflicting data, alternative interpretations and information will usually be dismissed as heretical. It can sometimes take one or more successive generations to come to examine and accept alternative explanations. Conflict will stimulate the patterns that seek to preserve and enhance our egos, our self-images. Our egos are formed and bounded by patterns. An ego is defined by what and who you *think* you are. Patterns dictate your values, beliefs and perceptions.

Collective patterns define our culture, which limits the way we perceive our relationship to the world. Astronomers at the time of Galileo refused even to look through his telescope. Their knowledge of the universe said that the earth was at its center and that any evidence to the contrary was obviously wrong and heretical. Physicians in the 1860s, who defended their understanding of medicine, refused to believe that microorganisms existed and that bacteria caused diseases and infections. As the 19th century ended, many prominent scientists believed that heavier-than-air ships, space flight and instant telecommunications were impossibilities. Serious consideration was given to the prospect of closing the US Patent Office because "everything had already been invented". Collective patterns and those patterns within you constrain you to view 'reality' through the patterns' filters and to feel uncomfortable when presented with alternate views.

Patterns cause you to continue to use your intellect to attempt to understand emotions, but your emotions lie outside of the realm of your intellect. In order to preserve itself, a pattern will cause you to believe that patterns do not exist by making you focus only on their effects – the repetitive lousy relationships, the chronic, nagging fears and addictions and the story that you are living now. You never really question what causes those effects, because you focus only on the patterns' tracks in your consciousness that are made by the patterns in your invisible unconscious.

You will be 'tagged' over and over by the patterns' graffiti until you destroy the invisible tagger itself. Now that you know what is causing your problem, your intellect will insist that following the tracks into the unknown will lead to the tagger. Good luck. May you get an amazing high-def video of Big Foot along the way as well.

We assume that the boundaries of our knowledge will keep expanding and give us information about the unknown areas that confront us. Although our body of knowledge is increasing at an exponential rate, it appears that the unknowns that are generated at the new boundaries become larger and more numerous. To compound the problem, everything without exception is continuously changing. That means that the assumptions that underlie every body of knowledge must be re-examined and verified. For example, medicine is examining the role that emotions and the mind-body connection play in causing diseases and alleviating suffering. However, doing so will trigger a defensive pattern in many, if not all, of the researchers because the patterns are defending themselves.

Now consider your imagination for a moment. Your imagination can easily show you things that are impossible in the physical world: a conversation with a long-dead historical figure, an instantaneous trip to the far side of the universe, hovering above a mountain and making invisible, non-physical objects appear visible – anything you ask for is possible. The imagination is unlimited and infinite in its scope. It is the source of all plans, goals, techniques and inventions. Your imagination is the opposite of your intellect; it is 'uneducated', playful, spontaneous, and infinite and does its work effortlessly. Like the mythical genie in the magic lamp, all you have to do is ask your imagination for something, and it will produce it while you watch passively. And you are in complete control of your imagination, which exists in the unconscious – along with the patterns that block your claims to peace, joy and understanding. You are in complete control of your infinitely versatile and powerful imagination, a tool that can be used to deal with an invisible pattern where it exists. Remember, a pattern can do only one thing – survive – and cannot think.

In summary, your intellect cannot rid you of the patterns' torment. The intellect resides in the left brain, whose perceptions are filtered through the patterns, which exist in the right-brain unconscious. Your thoughts themselves are filtered through the patterns, which have only their survival as their sole operating principle. As you will soon learn for yourself in the chapter on Free Will, Free Choice and Patterns, how you do not even control your own thoughts. This appears to be a heck of a fix to be in, but we will show you a very easy, quick and direct route to your senses of inner peace and joy that you have been seeking.

Feeling Trapped During Pregnancy All Better

Kim was a tall, attractive 34-year-old mother of a two-year-old boy and two months pregnant with her second child. It was a planned pregnancy. Initially she and her husband, Dillon, were very excited. However, for some unknown reason, Kim's joy collapsed into anxiety that overtook her. I only needed to see her for one session to be of assistance.

"Whenever my thoughts focus on being pregnant, 'something' takes over and scares me. I feel stuck in my head whenever I get this fear regarding the commitment I've made in having this baby. This fear makes me feel trapped. All I hear inside is 'one more commitment.' Commitment's the buzzword that takes over my life. Oh, and I know where it all originated. It came from a jerk I dated fourteen years ago. He got to me then and made me question myself, and I began to doubt myself. I know that doesn't make sense. Let me see if I can spell out better what happened in that dark relationship with him."

"That's not necessary Kim. I have more than enough information to help you get rid of that tormenting fear. Actually, I didn't even need to hear the story of how this anxiety came about nor the history of how you believe it began. All that information only allows the pattern to grip you even tighter with fear which you were probably feeling relating your story. Reliving your history only feeds the pattern and makes it stronger."

"I never thought of that before."

"I don't think many other people have either."

"How can I ever stop those fearful thoughts that come into my head?"

"I'll show you how. Let's began now. Reflect on a memory when this trapped and stuck feeling was the most intense and let me know when you have ones."

"Got it."

"As you observe it in your mind's eye, put a value of a number from one-to-ten on that upsetting memory. The higher the number, the more intense it feels."

"Oh, it's most definitely a ten."

I remotely lit up her central pathway with gold light. After each time I did so, I asked her to rate the number of its intensity. It eventually dropped to a one and stayed there. My outcome was a zero, so I enlisted her imagination's observance of the same situation in a symbolic image.

"Tell your imagination that you need its help. Do so within your own thoughts and not aloud."

"Did it."

Now, ask your imagination, and not yourself, to give you some image, symbol, character, person, monster, etc. is the one creating your fear."

"It's a monster of sorts. Very mean."

"Make yourself twenty, fifty or a hundred times bigger than the monster."

"OK."

"Ask the monster, 'What is your purpose in making me feel stuck and trapped while carrying this baby?'"

"It tries to attack me!"

IMAGINE ALL BETTER

"You don't need anything in your imagination that tries to harm you. So annihilate it. Kill it."

"I shot it."

"Is it dead?"

"I shot it six more times to make sure."

"Now, how would you like to feel instead of being so stressed out and trapped over the pregnancy?"

"Relaxed."

"Good. Now ask you imagination for it, and not you, to come up with the most positive image with the most positive energy that can reconnect you back to feeling relaxed."

"It's a big teddy bear. You know, all cuddly and soft."

"Ask it if it is here to help you feel relaxed and look forward to having your baby."

"It smiles."

"Now welcome it to come inside your heart, your spirit and every cell in your body."

"Done deal."

"See if there's a skeptic, that is, some doubt about its ability to truly help you. If there is one, you will hear it, see it or sense that it is there."

"I'm not aware of one."

"If there is one, it can't contain itself and will appear again if somehow we've missed it. You can't make mistakes in your imagination. That concept doesn't exist in the right brain. Now go back to that original scenario of fear of being stuck and trapped, and see if there is any emotional energy still attached to it. If so, let me know what number it is."

"It's at a four."

As I lit up her central pathway again the numbers dropped to a three, then a two, but didn't move beyond a two.

"OK. There is still something keeping you from feeling totally relaxed. That would be a pattern holding on for dear life - its life - at your life's expense. It's time for your imagination to come to the rescue! Ask your imagination for it to come up with an image, cartoon character, person, etc., that won't let you be free from that fearful emotion and be more relaxed during your pregnancy."

"It a minion," she said while laughing. "It's running back and forth mocking me."

Just the fact an image is laughing and mocking her comes under the heading of an 'attitude" image, one of ten patterns that reside in the unconscious mind of the more than 7.1 billion people in the world. That is how connected we all are. We could have stopped here, and Kim could have annihilated the minion. However, sometimes when we have the pattern up against the ropes, I like the image to show its true colors for teaching purposes before it's annihilated.

"Ask the minion. 'What is your purpose gripping me with fear?'"

"It said. 'Because I can.'"

"Ask the minion, 'How does that benefit you personally making me so fearful?'"

"All I hear it say is the word, 'Power.'"

"'Power' and 'Because I can' responses are also among the ten responses that represent two patterns controlling you. It has all your power, and that leaves you with no power over the overwhelming emotions the pattern has attached to your thoughts of pregnancy, until now. Destroy it. Kill it. Get mad at it."

"I used the same gun and shot it."

"Now ask your imagination, and not you, to come up with the most positive image with the most positive energy that can reconnect you to feeling inner peace and relaxed again."

"Me in a field of flowers. Now I'm jumping into water and riding on a dolphin. Whee!"

"Ask that image if it is here to help you feel relaxed."

"It says, 'Yeah. We're here for you.'"

"Then welcome that entire image to come into your heart, your spirit and every cell in your body."

"Done."

"Now go back to the original memory we started with that triggered fear and stress and see what number it is now."

As Kim was doing that I began to light up her central pathway again.

"I got it. It's a two. No. It's more like a one."

I lit up her central pathway one more time. "And now, what number is it?"

"It's a zero."

"Let's double-check. Try to bring up the worrisome thoughts and feelings with the original memory you started with.

"I can't. I don't feel it."

We both laughed.

"Can you describe what you are aware of now?"

"It feels like a release. I can now feel my body's energy flowing, like a river of energy flowing… whatever that means. It's like somebody could be telling me about their story that is similar to what mine was. I can relate to their story, but I cannot feel any negative feelings or emotions whatsoever. All those crazy-making thoughts are totally gone. What a relief."

"Great. Check in with me tomorrow and let me know how you're doing."

The next day Kim told me, "I slept like a baby last night."

Imagine All Better offers you freedom.

11

The Origins of Patterns

"Stresses you long ago forgot on the conscious level are still sending out signals, like buried microchips, making you anxious, tense, fatigued, apprehensive, resentful, doubtful, disappointed—these reactions cross the mind-body barrier to become a part of you."

— DEEPAK CHOPRA

HISTORY REVEALS THAT patterns have operated since time began. Patterns have convinced even the brightest minds to be tricked into and to defend false beliefs and out-and-out lies. Isaac Singer, winner of the Nobel Prize for literature in 1978, said: "A person is his own worst enemy....Ten enemies can't do what a person does to himself." Even a pattern in Gandhi gained more power by convincing him, "My most formidable opponent is a man named Mohandas K. Gandhi. With him I seem to have very little influence." Patterns are as omnipresent as the air we breathe and the water we drink.

The following three sources of patterns, coupled with our lack of awareness of their existences, make it impossible for any of us to go through our entire lives free of patterns. Remember that you are not your patterns. Patterns are energetic parasites in the same way that ticks, fleas and intestinal worms are physical parasites. However, once you become aware of a pattern, you can use the Imagine All Better approach described throughout this book to destroy the pattern simply, quickly and permanently.

Patterns begin their operations within you by three routes: inheritance, childhood and environment:

Inheritance. In 1983, Dr. Barbara McClintock was awarded the Nobel Prize in Physiology and Medicine for her discovery that genes migrate along chromosomes in response to stress. Patterns can be handed down to us through our genetic programming. Wars, famine, enslavement, genocide, plague, disease, floods and mass migration characterize human history. All of these serious events are recorded in the genes of those who experience them. Sickle-cell anemia, hemophilia and Tay-Sachs syndrome are examples of genetic diseases. In some cases, the emotions associated with these catastrophes are passed down to succeeding generations. Ancient fears and feuds have current meaning and are expressed in the stories such as those told in modern-day Turkey of Alexander the Great's invasion in 334 BCE and in the Middle East of the Crusades, which began in 1096 AD.

First Grader Being Bullied All Better

Diane called me and said that she was worried about her daughter, a first grader, who was being picked on at school. Diane started worrying about her daughter's situation from the time she awoke in the morning, and her anxiety rose at she dropped her daughter off at school. Diane said that she, herself, had been bullied by her classmates at a similar age, and that she did not wish her daughter to experience the same treatment. She reported that the intensity of her worry was an eight on a zero-to-10 scale.

It was clear to me that, unless the bullying pattern in Diane was removed, her daughter would continue to experience bullying because her daughter was absorbing the pattern's energy from Diane.

I asked Diane's imagination to come up with an image that represented the bully and to destroy it. She then called upon her imagination to produce an image that represented confidence and calm. Diane absorbed the energy from the confident and calm image without any trace of any skeptic or doubt. In checking her worry about her daughter, the intensity of the worry fell from an eight to a four and then a zero as I remotely lit up her central pathway with gold light each time after the number of the intensity of her reported numbers dropped.

Next I asked Diane to work with an image of her daughter and asked that image what her intensity was regarding being bullied. Her daughter's image replied that the intensity was an eight. I lit up Diane's central pathway and she reported that her daughter's image said that the intensity fell rapidly to a zero. I was confident that the bullying patterns in both Diane and her daughter were permanently destroyed.

Diane called me two weeks later to report that she no longer felt any worry about her daughter's treatment when she drove her daughter to school. Her daughter said that her classmates no longer picked on her. Diane told me that these changes happened the very next day after she had destroyed the patterns. With the pattern's 'magnet' that attracted the resonant frequency of the bully now destroyed, the bully passes by her daughter as if she is invisible, and the bully seeks out the frequency of a bully pattern in another child at school. Imagine working with the collective unconsciousness of all the students in the entire school simultaneously and ending the collective pattern of any student's being bullied as well as the patterns within the bullies.

Childhood. Patterns can be acquired from caregivers, authority figures and peers from your childhood. As an infant, your brain wave state is such that you absorb the patterns, values and feelings of those closest to you. A family group is the environment where most childhood patterns are initiated and nurtured since this is where you, as an infant, absorb both the positive and negative energies of the people around you. Since every pattern begins its operation from the moment it takes up residence within you, you can become aware of a pattern's existence by being aware of the repetitive nature of the circumstances that you encounter. That is, when you realize that certain circumstances appear to repeat themselves in your life, you are observing the effects of a pattern's operation. For example, a person with a pattern of abuse from childhood will unconsciously attract abusive or manipulative relationships through adulthood. Once the pattern is destroyed, the energy from the abuse is no longer necessary to feed that pattern. The relationship between the person and the abuser will then be dramatically changed or ended.

Fear of Men All Better

Marilyn, age 48, was in and out of therapy over many years. She told me, "I've always had physical fear of men since I was a little girl… still do to a certain extent or I wouldn't have brought it up with you. I was never able to deal with it during several years of therapy with three different therapists, all of whom were very nice and sincere. I eventually understood *why* I had it, but I still had it. I believe that same physical fear had to do with my marriage failing. I found my husband to be a very difficult man to live with. We would have divorced if it wasn't for financial reasons so we separated, and have remained cordial and stay in touch."

I only needed to know the intensity of the emotions attached to her story of having physical fear of men on a zero-to-10 scale. It was a 10. As I lit up her central pathway with gold light, Marilyn reported her numbers collapsing to a five, a three and then a zero, upon which she said, "I'm very tired now." This indicated that a pattern was destroyed. When asked to conjure up that same fearful feeling associated with men, she could not find it at all any more.

We also addressed and completely resolved the intense emotions associated with numerous issues within three sessions over the telephone which Marilyn described as, "Not honoring my intuition, being late, martyr and victims issues, fighting with some part of myself, co-dependent in relationships, trying to change others, challenged trying to fix myself, attracting people who victimize me, holding back whenever getting close to my creative goals opening up, never good enough no matter what I do, and intimidated by computers and technology."

A couple of weeks later, she called and left a phone message: "I thought of something I wanted to tell you. Remember how we worked on that physical fear of men in our initial session and the major problems it created with my husband and me? Well, he has done a 180-degree turn. I don't know what happened. He's become *so* nice. He asks how I am. He's no longer horrible to be around. I don't know if it has anything to do with the work we did, but he has changed tremendously. And there's another man in my life that has also done a 180-degree turn in the way that he's behaving. Thought I'd share that with you. The two major men in my life have completely changed, and in a good way!"

Marilyn's logical mind could not comprehend how her chronic problem could be eliminated forever in a non-linear, non-logical manner and result in such a spontaneous, "miraculous" shift in her consciousness. On one level, she knew she felt better about having the male-energy issue resolved, but had not put two and two together until she verbalized the shift that had occurred. She could not fathom it had been removed simply by lighting up her central pathway while she focused on her fearful scenario with men who had disrupted her entire life.

I reminded her when we spoke a few days later that ever since her childhood, she had been viewing men through the filter of a pattern of fear. However, that repeating pattern is permanently destroyed, and as a result it can no longer press buttons in her estranged husband and the other gentleman. That dance has ended forever. She perceives men now as if she never had the original issue of fear. Hence, Marilyn's initial perception was that *they* had made a 180-degree turnabout. Everybody benefits whenever a ruling pattern has been dethroned.

Environment. Patterns also begin their operation within you as a result of significant events that can occur at any age. Examples of environmental patterns are post-traumatic stress disorder, long-term, persistent depression from a significant loss, phobias of assault or accident victims, fears related to the reaction of an authority figure and confining emotions connected with any other significant event at any time in your life. Patterns from the environment are frequently easier to identify than those from inheritance or childhood because you can frequently identify the event that caused the feeling. However, all patterns are resistant to conventional analyses.

Veteran's Post Traumatic Stress All Better

We knew Imagine All Better could do wonders for our veterans returning from Iraq and Afghanistan as well as the coalition troops from around the world who served there. However, the first vet with whom I worked was Sarge Lintecum, age 64, from Tempe, Arizona, who served three tours in Viet Nam during 1966, 1967 and 1968. He was highly decorated and received the Purple Heart.

Sarge lived a life of hell battling his demons for 19 years upon returning from his last tour in Viet Nam. The patterns that came back with him made him *appear* to sabotage himself over and over. At times, he was homeless. His emotional healing finally began with his writing poetry and novels about his experiences in Viet Nam. Another way he found he could turn off the internal chaos in his mind was to reach out and help other vets who were all but forgotten.

Sarge opened up about painful issues that have haunted him since the late 1960s. He said, "No vets are ever the same the remainder of their lives upon returning home. What happened in Nam shattered my self-image because of what I had to do by taking the lives of innocent people against every value and moral I was raised upon. I carried an M79 grenade launcher. One bullet weighed half a pound and was the size of an actual golf ball. It exploded when it hit something solid. The memory of a lady holding a baby being shredded upon impact still bothers me. For years, I could not look myself in the mirror. I still feel a lot of anxiety and heaviness in my chest since it occurred."

Sarge was asked to rate the emotional intensify of his anxiety and the heaviness in his chest on a scale of zero-to-10; the higher the number, the more intense the emotional and physical feelings. Sarge rated them an eight. While he focused on the memory associated with those feelings, I let up his central pathway with gold light. As he reported the numbers coming down, he commented, "I can only see the baby now, but no longer the woman." When he reported the number being a zero, I asked Sarge to see what feelings, if any, were still left with that memory. He said, "It slipped away like a bar of soap. Completely gone. Even the baby's image evaporated!"

There was another incident that happened when he spent months in the jungle where he was "made an accomplice to murder" without his knowledge. He said, "We had captured a prisoner, and we were taking him back. I was near the end of the column of some 30 soldiers while the prisoner was way up in the front when I heard the sound of a loud 'pop' coming from that direction. When I got up there, our Lieutenant walked us by the dead prisoner whom our South Vietnamese interrogator had shot in his third eye for not knowing the answers for his questions. It was not because he tried to escape either. We were marched by him while he was on the ground bleeding, and we were made an accessory to his murder. I have always had shame and resentment with these memories."

I asked him to put a number of the emotional intensity associated with being made an accomplice to murder on a zero-to-10 scale and received a 10. As I lit up Sarge's central pathway numerous times, his numbers dropped to an eight, a five, a three and then flat lined out at a zero. I had him double-check to see if there were any lingering feelings remaining, and none could be resurrected.

His response was, "I think I'm good. It was a clean hole in the third eye. I just don't like the murder. But I don't have any upsetting feelings."

We spoke many times over the next few years and became good friends. I asked him how he was doing regarding the issues we addressed, and he said, "It's still working. It's amazing to me. Every day my life had been ruled by PSTD, but I now stay out of this longer and longer than any time before. The feeling of anxiety and the heavy feeling in my chest didn't come back any more. It's like being on the computer, and I open up a folder. There's the document with the file attachments with anxiety and heavy chest feeling and those attachments are now totally removed. I've been trying all these years to get over the lady and the baby myself. And it's gone now. I'm not proud of being an accomplice to murder either, but I don't feel it like I did before. I'm OK now."

Sarge has become a beacon of light for veterans' rights. He and his lovely wife, Leslie, have become instrumental helping vets from every era to receive disability benefits they deserve for injuries and PTSD. [Information can be found at www.vietnamblues.com]

Once a pattern begins its operation, your perceptions and reactions become automatic and you rarely, if ever, questioned them. Your ego, who you *think* you are, then absorbs the perceptions and reactions, and the pattern makes you resist questioning your perceptions and reactions because the questions feel like a personal attack. You mistakenly believe that you, and the patterns are one. And so the patterns use you to defend them.

Imagine All Better offers you freedom.

12

Patterns' Unlimited Activites

"How you do one thing is how you do everything."

— Anonymous Eastern saying

A PATTERN DOES NOT limit itself to a particular area of your life. Like a paper cut on a finger, which is always in the least convenient spot, or a stubbed toe, which affects your entire posture and gait, a pattern affects every aspect of your perception and behavior. When something is not functioning in a relationship, then your entire perspective is undermined. For example, a difficult relationship with a boss becomes a thorn in your side that colors your relationships at home, with friends and those you encounter in the course of your life. A pattern from your childhood, such as mistrust of authority figures, affects how you view your chances for success in all areas of your life. Relationship difficulties with your parents will affect your relationships with spouses, significant others, children, coworkers and bosses.

Destroying a pattern that causes you frustration with someone's behavior will result in improvement in another, seemingly unrelated facet of your life. Imagine patterns forming a three-dimensional energy web that limits your perceptions, plays with your emotions and controls your behavior. When you destroy one of those patterns, the shape of that entire web will shift because one of the nodes or knots in the web has been removed. The entire structure is weakened when one of its elements is removed and your entire life benefits.

The Eastern saying: "How you do one thing is how you do everything" means that the level of your awareness or presence to what is happening in the moment operates in all facets of your life. You become present to what is happening in the moment when you annihilate a pattern and take back the emotional energy that you unknowingly fed it. The energy that you recoup is now yours in the form of 'presence' that enhances your ability to stay present in the moment in all situations. If you are not present to what is happening in the moment, then the pattern's operations will determine how you behave in, perceive and relate to every situation.

A pattern is energy, and all energy has an associated frequency. Therefore, a pattern's frequency, its influence, permeates everything within and around you. Much like a radio wave – a specific frequency – that passes through your body, a pattern's frequency affects the way you perceive and react to your world. Every pattern that you carry affects *all* of your perceptions, reactions and emotions. You cannot say that a given pattern isolates itself to a specific area of your life. Like the cell phone in your hand and the electrical waves from your heart, a pattern's presence is detectable throughout your entire psychological and physical makeup.

How Patterns Affect the Body

The notion of frequency is accompanied by the concept of resonance. Resonance occurs when two objects vibrate at the same frequency or some whole multiple of each other's frequencies. Consider two stretched guitar strings that are separated by some distance and are of the same length or a whole multiple of each other's length. When one guitar string is struck the distant other string will begin to vibrate. This is an example of resonance between the two guitar strings. Other examples of resonance are the receiver circuits in radios, televisions and cell phones. The circuits in those devices are tuned to a resonant frequency of the transmitter, which is sending a signal. The resonant circuit in the receiving device vibrates with the transmitted signal and passes the received signal to an amplifier, and the amplified signal is finally displayed as a video, picture, voice or text message. Resonance allows us to communicate with satellites, space probes and roving vehicles on Mars. We use expressions such as: "I'm in synch with you.", "That idea resonates with me.", and " I get good vibes from her."

Everything, including thoughts, is composed of energy. Every disease, physical dysfunction and psychological state has a unique frequency associated with it. A resonant frequency for a dysfunctional or unhealthy condition will correspond to those of an emotion or group of emotions. Consider how you feel when you are in the early stage of an infection such as a cold or flu, or after eating spoiled food. Note your emotional reactions upon hearing about a young child's death, or your feeling "bad" when a friend tells you of her illness or injury.

All illnesses have an accompanying emotional content. In many cases, persons with an illness are not aware of their emotions associated with their illness. And even if they are aware of an emotion, they believe it is natural to feel worry, fear and despair because of their illness. They accept the emotion without question. This is because those emotions are attached by a pattern to an illness or physical limitation on an unconscious level. Destroying a pattern associated with an illness or physical limitation assists in restoring health and balance. The bodymind is able to perform at its optimal level when the associated upsetting emotions are removed. We define balance as just the right amount of physical or emotional energy needed to optimize a situation.

Patterns generate conditions that lead to symptoms receiving a diagnosis with difficult or nonexistence treatments. Lupus, Epstein Barr, fibromyalgia and the controversial Asperger's syndrome are such perplexing conditions. By addressing and destroying the patterns associated with such conditions, a dramatic shift takes place that opens awareness of other patterns to be destroyed. Within a short interval, the symptoms of these illnesses are replaced with a feeling of balance. Minimally, negative emotions that are generated by patterns' activities aggravate *any* condition. Anyone with diabetes will experience effects on insulin levels when in stressful situations.

Justin's Asperger's Manifestation All Better

Linda's eight-year-old son, Justin, had fears that were controlling him for several years. She said, "Justin has been diagnosed with a mild form of autism known as Asperger's syndrome. He's had serious sleeping problems for several years and for that reason we've had him in psychotherapy. He is obsessed that we'll be robbed. His preoccupation with burglars' breaking into our house has made him so fearful that his father and I have moved out of our master suite upstairs and into the bedroom next to his to make him feel more secure. No matter how many times we reassure him that he is safe, and we are here to protect him, his anxiety has a mind of its own."

Two days later, an endearing Justin appeared at my office. I found him to be highly verbal and vividly descriptive of his problem. He talked quickly about many issues that may have been viewed as fragmented and nonsensical. His disjointed pieces of information included his description of the problem: "fearful of robbers," "bad people," "sleepless nights," etc., as well as his images of the problem: "an old lady who inhabits my closet," "piercing red eyes of the old lady," "a clown and juggler at the end of my bed who wouldn't go away," and "a skeleton on a skateboard." Insightfully, Justin verbalized what many children feel but cannot express: "I feel sorry for myself."

When I walked Justin through his imagination, his imagination presented him an image of a robber wearing a mask that was making him have his sleeping problems. When he asked the robber's intention, the robber said, "I want your valuables." When Justin questioned him further, the robber's bottom line intent was simply, "I am mean." I instructed Justin to annihilate the mean robber's image. Justin went into an elongated description of how powerful transformer action toys and cartoon champions succeeded "in taking the robber out." A guard dog spontaneously appeared when Justin was asked to invite an "all better" image that would make him feel protected. Immediately, Justin proclaimed with a big warm smile, "I feel safe."

The second process that we addressed was another character, an old lady with red eyes who came out of his closet at night and scared him. When asked her intention in behaving in this frightening manner, she had a few bizarre responses such as, "Old ladies are like this," and "I want to help you take over the world." Justin did not like nor trust this old lady's menacing image, so he called upon many of his friendly cartoon characters to annihilate her. After her demise, like the death of the Wicked Witch in the Wizard of Oz, it opened a 'space' in Justin's imagination that the symbolic image of the old lady no longer occupied. His imagination then gave him another image that would be helpful. Justin said, "It's the strong man from circus," who said, "Your wish is my command." Justin quickly viewed the strong man as a 'show off.' "I've gotten a much better one!" he exclaimed. "It's Hercules." When asked how he felt about Hercules, Justin approvingly said, "Safe, of course." Justin welcomed Hercules to come inside him as an ally.

The last process that day was the evil skeleton on the skate board. Justin said, "He just wants to keep me very scared." When Justin's imagination was enlisted, it presented an image Justin called his "friend". It was Tony Hawk, the world- champion skateboarder, who proceeded to run over and destroy the skeleton figure. Justin invited Tony's image to enter his heart, spirit and body. He then added, "I feel *proud* that I have a hero like him in my house."

When Justin and his mother returned for a follow-up session, he reported, "I've had the best night's sleep in my whole life." His mother concurred. Justin continued to sleep well, much to the delight of his parents who returned to their own bedroom. Justin's fears disappeared as quickly as they had appeared. Months later, I had the pleasure of meeting Justin again and learned not only was he sleeping consistently, but he had become a singer and guitar player in his own rock band. He went on to entertain me with one of his songs he had written and also sang some of Alicia Keys' songs. He was capable of remembering every word to every song that he ever heard – or anything he had ever read! Justin was not as surprised as I was with such a feat. He proudly said, "You know I'm nine now." I replied, "That answers everything," while applauding his performance. He was the most delightful and vibrant person I have ever met.

Imagine All Better offers you freedom.

13

Pattern Interactions

"Mental illness is a kind of amnesia, in which the patient has forgotten his own powers."

— COLIN WILSON

HISTORY REVEALS HOW patterns can pit family member against family member, countrymen against countrymen, and take down world leaders, CEOs of corporations, politicians in high places, and even religious leaders. Nobody is immune from the operations of patterns, but everybody has the capability to destroy patterns.

An approval-seeking pattern is present in each of us, and allows us to become members of families, tribes, religions, clubs, political parties and any organization. As children, our conforming to the expectations of our families helps to ensure our survival. You will learn to agree at a very early age that the "emperor's new clothes are magnificent" even though you can see clearly that he is naked. Your disagreement will result in some form of punishment. The rewards that you get for agreeing with and practicing the "rules" rapidly reinforce the approval-seeking pattern within you — and in those who maintain the rules. The approval-seeking pattern permits stable business structures to exist through conscious and unconscious rules of etiquette regarding how you deal with authority.

Business organizations ensure conformity to their rules by means of performance reviews, giving annual salary increases, awarding year-end bonuses, acknowledging tasks well done, granting promotions and threatening job loss. As a result, much organizational energy goes into maintaining the status quo. The real, unconscious objective of all those time-wasting, mind-numbing meetings is the reinforcement of approval-seeking patterns, not the building of consensus. After all, consensus means agreement among a group, which means that everyone in the group has both given and received approval in some form.

Moreover, the inherited pattern of seeking approval will cause organizations to ignore or discount significant changes in their business areas. If the business leader does not see the threatening change and deal with it because of a pattern within the leader, then the subordinate employees will conform to the leader's views. The lower-level employees who do see the threat and choose to share their views will be perceived as threats themselves. The alarmists' behaviors threaten the approval-seeking patterns in others, particularly the patterns within the leadership. The leaders' resulting upsetting emotions will cause the leaders to get the offenders to conform to the leaders' views by — you guessed it – withholding approval.

Therefore, real change has the best chance of occurring when it starts at the top of any organization. Destroying the limiting patterns within the leadership has a profound effect not only on the leaders but also on those throughout the organization. Everyone is exquisitely attuned from birth to the values, attitudes and behaviors of authority figures. Organizations are intricate, energetic webs of pattern interactions. The principle nodes within those webs are the patterns within the leaders. A change within a leader guarantees a change within the entire organization. Externally focused concepts such as reengineering, reorganizing, team building, flow charting, supply-chain management, strategic planning, zero-based budgeting, six-sigma design, customer service, etc. are useful, but truly meaningful change can come only from destroying limiting patterns.

Decision makers have failed to see patterns even in situations where their lives, and the lives of their organizations were threatened. The Vikings, who brought Christianity to Greenland, lived on sheep and cattle. As the climate changed, the meadows shrank and the number livestock dwindled along with the size of the meadows. However, the natives were thriving by eating the fish, whales and sea vegetables that were found in abundance. The natives pointed out that the Vikings could feed themselves very well by fishing. The Vikings responded to their rising population and shrinking food supply by building bigger churches, and the Vikings starved in the midst of abundance. Because the patterns within them blinded them to viable options, the Vikings were unable to see or consider the option of fishing.

Digital Equipment Corporation (DEC) was a highly successful and innovative manufacturer of many computers in the 1960s and 70s. DEC was the largest employer in Massachusetts, second to the state government. DEC's executives refused to believe that the 32-bit desktop computer posed a threat to their business and never developed a product line to meet that challenge. DEC's sales nose-dived, and Compaq swallowed DEC in 1998. Subsequently, Hewlett-Packard swallowed Compaq. The patterns within DEC blinded the organization to the technology changes that were transforming the industry.

Minolta was an admired and innovative company that introduced the first auto- focusing single-lens-reflex film camera in the 1980s. Industry experts told Minolta in the early 1990s that photography would shift from film media to all-digital and by 2000 the transition would be well underway. The patterns within Minolta executives caused them to ignore the experts' correct advice and instead develop a new film format with a huge research, development and advertising expenditure. This was a path that did not threaten the patterns' existences. The emotional and financial price the executives, employees and shareholders paid for the blunder kept the patterns living off their emotional anxiety, guilt and blaming themselves for all they lost. The new format failed; Minolta did not have the resources to compete in the new digital age and subsequently had to exit the camera business completely in 2006.

Whenever businesses - and other organizations - continue to ignore patterns, they are doomed to extinction. If businesses do not kill patterns within them, then the patterns will kill the businesses!

Individual Pattern Interactions

You quickly become aware of others' reactions in terms of their likes and dislikes, preferences and aversions, as well as their complete set of 'hot buttons'. You will quickly adjust your behavior, consciously or unconsciously, to the reactions that you observe in those around you. In particular, you will adjust your behavior to the reactions in the executives and managers in your workplace. All managers unconsciously teach their organizations what the managers want to hear and how they want to hear it. An executive's directive to "think outside the box" is one that will produce strong reactions in all those involved. Any change will be met with some degree of resistance because one or more patterns will feel a threat to its existence. Any change will be perceived as a threat to the perceived authority that management has over the outcome from an existing, known process. Executives, managers and others involved with an existing process have patterns within them that are concerned with "saving face." A new and unknown process represents a threat to the self-images with everyone involved.

Businesses and government organizations have responded to the need for change by looking outside themselves. They hire consultants who show them different, more efficient communication methods, reengineering strategies, different performance-improvement methods and incentive-reward programs. However, all of the options for change that are offered and selected are those that do not threaten the existence of the patterns within the executives and managers because all of the methods are externally focused. However, unless the limiting patterns within the leadership are destroyed by an internally focused method, nothing substantial will change. Real change can only happen from the top down because the senior executives are those who have the ultimate power, authority and influence to direct and approve what options are acceptable.

In your workspace, you apply judgment based upon the operation of the patterns within you. You may claim that performance evaluations and "360 reviews" provide objective measures for employees as well as organizational performances. However, there is no value measure, emotion or rank attached to any behavior, object, profit or condition. You may apply a favorable assessment to a situation, while someone else would find this same situation to be deplorable. You find the glass half full, the other finds the glass half empty. You find plenty of indications for optimism. Someone else finds many pessimistic indicators. There is no objectivity. There can be no objectivity. It is the patterns that cause you to believe in the illusion of objectivity. Everything is subjective at all times.

You must still make judgments or appraisals that are necessary to support a process. However, you must remember that because every moment is unique and can never be duplicated, every situation and event is unlike any other situation and event although there may be similarities. Patterns cause you to believe that situations and events are identical, when they can be only similar. Therefore, there can be no cookbook or one-size-fits-all rule that can be used to make assessments in all situations. Every situation and event requires that you consider it in the moment of its occurrence. A pattern prevents you from being fully present to what is happening in the moment and perceiving the unique aspects of every situation. When you destroy a pattern, you remove the filter that prevented you from seeing other options, and you have access to a wider set of choices.

All patterns require emotional energy to exist. You unknowingly supply patterns with your emotional energy that comes from your reaction to events such as anniversaries of losses, situations such as one that reminds you of a difficult time and others' upsetting behaviors. Others' behaviors are, in turn, motivated by patterns, which are triggered by the behaviors induced by the patterns in you. It is like a tennis match that will continue nonstop until one player decides to no longer participate and destroys the pattern. When a pattern in you that presses your button is finally destroyed, the pattern in other person can no longer evoke that upsetting emotion in you. That particular emotional volleying between you and the other person is over. Your relationship with the other person will be changed significantly, since the energy flow between the patterns has been terminated.

One of my neighbors, Megan, who was originally from Ireland, told me that she was returning to Ireland for a family reunion, but was debating doing so because of her older sister Erin has pressed her buttons since they were children. She said, "She's always been mean to me. I hate her!" I told her there was no need for her to miss the family reunion because I could show her how to delete the buttons her sister presses in her. She agreed, although she was highly skeptical.

I asked Megan to recollect an intense memory of her sister pressing her buttons. She said she got one that "really pisses me off". She ranked it on a zero-to-10 scale and gave it a rating of 10 plus. I lit up her central pathway with gold light while she held onto that upsetting memory and it dropped immediately to a one, and then to a zero.

I saw Megan while I was walking my dog a few weeks after she had returned from Ireland. She said was dumbfounded. "My sister was no longer the sister I've known. I had no idea who she was anymore! She was kind, consistent, generous and warm. I started to get pissed off when I felt manipulated by her getting all of us in the family to toss in some money for her daughter's upcoming graduation gift. Somehow, I didn't lose it like I usually would have. The next day Erin called me and apologized for not having asked me if that was okay regarding my putting money toward her daughter's gift. Bottom line, I had a great time with my family."

Everyone has a set of unique reactions, or quirks, to similar situations. You feel comfortable with others when the patterns in you and the patterns in others respond to each other with complementary energy. That is why you are attracted to persons, situations and careers in which patterns in you and those in the others around you are complementary. Members of political, social or religious organizations hold similar beliefs and therefore feel comfortable in each other's company because patterns are not being activated. When group members encounter a group with differing or opposing views, the result of the patterns' interactions between the two groups will be feelings of discomfort, ridicule, antagonism, defensiveness and general unease.

Patterns trigger your perception that others are with you or against you. You will find that anyone or anything that challenges or negates a pattern within you makes you uncomfortable, and you will want to remove yourself from that person or situation. For example, you may dislike your job, but no aspect of your job, in and of itself, has an emotion attached to it. It is your *perception* and *interpretation* of your job that are the results of the patterns' activity causing your dissatisfaction. Whatever or whoever bothers you at work does not necessarily bother another coworker. The interactions of the patterns within you and the patterns of those with whom you deal cause the negative emotions that you associate with your job. A typical workplace is a stage on which groups of patterns within employees interact with and reinforce the patterns within each other by triggering emotional reactions. Some resulting typical emotions associated with a job are fear of losing the job, hostility toward job duties, resentment of coworkers' status and salary inequality.

In the case of patterns, likes, and not opposites, attract. In fact, opposite patterns never attract each other, but remain invisible to each other and cannot press each others' buttons. Consider an example of the attraction between a society debutante and an ex-con biker, the classic nice girl - bad boy 'romance'. The patterns in each partner seek each other through the coin analogy. The nice girl wishes to be free of social conventions, and the bad boy symbolizes a mocking of social conventions. The couple's behaviors represent two sides of the same coin – the spectrum from social leader to social outsider

Making Cold Calls All Better

Kyle, age 44, "hated" making telephone calls. His job was in Florida for a national insurance company. Due to the shift in the U.S. economy since 2008 together with the depressed real estate market and high unemployment in Florida, he lost his former drive to excel.

"I hate making cold calls on the phone. I have such resistance. It's hard to motivate my team with my energy tied up."

"How would you like to feel instead of your energy been drained making these calls?"

"Positive. Having curiosity over the outcome of the calls. Comfortable and confident."

When he asked his imagination for an image making him hate making cold calls, the first one that manifested was an uncle who proceeded to lambaste him by lecturing him and pointing his finger at Kyle. What had manifested was a pattern we call an 'accusatory' one. He was asked to destroy it by turning the uncle's image into a fragile glass statue and imagine a boulder falling from the sky and shattering it to pieces. Kyle then asked his imagination for a positive image that would make him feel positive, comfortable and confident, and said, "Me on my motorcycle popped into my mind immediately. It's my BMW with me on it, taking tight twisting turns, gearing down, leaning the bike over more and more and more while the bike cuts into corners."

When asked to see if there was a skeptic making him feel he could not be confident making calls, an image of his father showed up. His father ended up lecturing him as well! He imagined his father's image as if it were a photograph or piece of film and put a match to it and reported its being ashes. When he asked him imagination for an image that would make him feel confident and comfortable making cold calls he said, "It's me greeting somebody with a firm handshake." When asked how he felt looking at the image he said he had, "High confidence."

I asked Kyle to come up with a memory at work in which he hated making cold calls, and he immediately had one. I then asked him, "On a zero-to-10 scale, where zero is your feeling completely comfortable and confident looking at that memory now, and as the numbers increase, it means your experiencing intense resistance and hatred for making cold calls. Rank what number that emotional intensity is as you look at that frustrating scenario at work." He reported the number being a five. I lit up his central pathway with gold light each time he told me the numbers became lower. However, it wouldn't drop any lower than a one. I told him to ask his imagination to give him an image making him hate making cold calls. He got an image of "a jumble of faces". He was then told to ask the "jumble of faces" if any of them were on his side to help him feel comfortable making cold calls to take two steps forward. Many faces did so, but several stayed behind. He was instructed to destroy the ones that stayed behind. He came up with a ball of fire from a flamethrower and used it to destroy the images of the non-supporting faces.

I said, "As you look at the images that came forward, thank them and tell them to transform themselves into the most positive image with the most positive energy that reconnects you to feel confident while making cold calls." Kyle said, "They are now in agreement. I can now see them clearly. I couldn't before. Each of them separated from being one collective image of faces into eight individual persons' images. They make me smile."

"Imagine that image going right inside your body. It knows how to communicate with you on a cellular level. Check to see whether or not there are any skeptics for those images."

"None."

"Go back to that zero-to-10 scale and let me know what number that original intensity of hatred and resistance toward cold calling is now."

"It's zero. I can do this fine. This is good."

"Double-check if there is any remnant of negative feelings still remaining with making the calls."

"No. I feel very complete. It has nothing to do with phones anymore... just the general situation in terms of what I'm doing for an occupation. It sucks trying to make my job work. My approach is pragmatic. It's either working or not working, and the stress at my job is not working. It's depressing." And so we addressed and resolved his feeling of being depressed in a similar way.

Several days later, I received a call from Kyle who said, "The litmus test was Monday morning doing what I hated the most. Monday morning rolled around and I was able to be proactive. I had no issues and started dialing one number after another number non-stop. My love-hate relationship had turned into a mission of being driven to do vs. hating to do cold calls. What kept coming up in my mind was a boost of confidence with the image of the bike rider doing what I loved to do the most – twisting and turning on roads. The rider represented confidence and control. And my production went up."

Suggestions Cannot Change a Pattern

My favorite waitress, Nora, was complaining about her daughters, ages 14 and 17, who were using their cell phones and texting all the time, especially during the family evening meals. She told them their behavior upset her because she felt if was disrespectful. I asked her who paid their cell phone bills. Nora said that she did it to help them out. I told her she already had the solution to a problem bugging her, and it would allow her to have more money as she was complaining about how tight her finances were. It was like Nora had never connected the dots before. She neither introduced any alternatives nor acknowledged my suggestion of her terminating their cell phones.

The patterns in Nora kept her feeling angry, frustrated and disrespected. The patterns of anger, frustration and disrespect in turn were feeding the addiction patterns in her daughters. In turn, the patterns in her daughters fueled the patterns in Nora - like a dog chasing its tail. Did Nora ever take any action? Never. The story with which she identified was that of a martyr, a victim. It permeated her conversations with friends, family and customers: "Look how good I am and how people take advantage of me." And thus the patterns grow stronger. And unless the patterns in Nora are annihilated, she will find herself in more situations in which she plays the role of a martyr. She will unknowingly live the martyr role in her story, her self-image.

Imagine All Better offers you freedom.

14

Social Media: A Feeding Frenzy For Patterns

"The purpose of poetry is to remind us that there are no doors and windows, and that uninvited guests come in and out at will."

— MILOSZ CZESLAW, POET

NOT VERY LONG ago, our interactions occurred at a much slower pace than they do now. There was more time to be alone with our thoughts to reflect on the day's interactions. Commuting and time outside the workplace provided opportunities for reflection and chances for developing an insight to patterns in our lives. However, modern instant messaging and social media have greatly reduced reflective time. The Internet, Facebook, Twitter, Instagram, smartphones, and texting have changed our world forever and, like everything in our dual-natured universe, have brought benefits and accompanying costs.

The cost of instant messaging and social media is the feeding and strengthening of the patterns at an ever-increasing rate with a huge price tag. That price tag includes:

- Deterioration of attention to family members' emotional needs and interactions, and the resulting destruction of family cohesiveness;
- A decline in academic performance, writing, composition and critical-thinking skills;
- An inability to filter significant information from the trivial;
- A marked retardation in developing social skills because face-to-face interactions have declined;
- The sharing of highly personal information and photographs that will become highly embarrassing material for future relationships and job prospects;
- An end to quiet time for inner reflection and rejuvenation;
- In many cases, sleep is being interrupted and curtailed, which will cause fatalities or injuries caused by distracted drivers and pedestrians;
- Teenagers' suicides and
- Lost productivity when employees surf the net and use social media while on the job.

The news is filled with numerous examples of how the use of communication media reinforces the patterns. An extreme example is a teenager's suicide that is induced by numerous negative messages sent to the teenager. The young suicide victim interprets those messages according to the pattern within him or her, which induces the feelings of depression and despair. Another example is a fatality caused by a person who is engineering a locomotive or driving an automobile while speaking on a cell phone or texting. In some cases, family interactions are seriously harmed when parents and children are simultaneously engaged in surfing the Internet, reading emails and texting. The parents' attention, which is vital to their children's development, is constantly interrupted, weakened or eliminated when the parents' attention is diverted for extended intervals. Using instant-messaging devices in the classroom greatly detracts from students' attention and understanding the lesson material.

These escalating issues result because instant messaging, texting, cell-phone use and voicemail allow you to send and receive messages at ever-increasing speed. Patterns in others demand that you are constantly available to receive the messages and respond immediately regardless of where you are, what you are doing or what time of day or night it is. When you do not bring awareness into your use of these media, you will use your reactions to the messages, such as pressure, anger, worry, frustration and fear to trigger the crazy-making patterns in you and those who receive your replies. If chosen without awareness, the words that you use to reply will be those that the patterns in you force you to use. All of your interactions will cost some level of emotional energy, which will be used to reinforce the patterns that generated that emotion in the first place. The messages themselves carry no emotional content; your patterns cause you to apply an emotional tone to your interactions.

Messages that contain emotions with more emotional charge include those with abusive or strong language, sexual references and explicit photographs. Most people do not believe that their undisciplined use of social media has become an addiction because they rationalize that since 'everyone is doing it', it is normal. If you believe that your use of social media, texting and instant messaging is not addictive, then see what happens if you were to give them up for one week. If your job requires you to stay connected, then make an agreement with your employer that, for one week, you will turn off your device after 6 PM and will turn it on again at 8 AM. Any takers out there? Of course not, because you have at least three 'titanium-clad' reasons why you could not possibly do this – or rather the patterns have given you those three great rationales to not do this. You have just observed how the patterns within you do an extremely clever job in providing the reasons to protect their operations. Maybe you thought that you had no addictions controlling your life! Sure.

There is, of course, nothing inherently wrong or bad with using social media, because the media and the messages are neutral. However, using social media must be accompanied by an awareness of patterns. Unless you can use awareness in these interactions, you are unintentionally reinforcing the patterns that cause you to use social media compulsively. Unless you destroy the patterns that your emotions are feeding when you use communication media, those patterns will demand more and more of your emotional energy. The consequence of your lack of awareness is a form of "energy addiction" to the use of communication media. Since a pattern cannot think, it does not know how much is enough and can never be satisfied. A pattern will cause you to devote more and more time and emotional energy to the pattern's ever-growing energy demands.

Distractions, Text Messaging and Bad Grades All Better

Erik telephoned me as soon as he arrived at college the beginning of his sophomore year. He was anxious not to repeat the mistakes he made during his freshman year when his grades were the worst he ever received. He had been an A-student in high school and graduated with a 4.1 GPA.

He said, "I have to keep clear of distractions this year to get A's. There's a lot of drama with text messaging every day that constantly interferes with my studying, my classes, and just about everything. Whenever I get a text message, I have to respond right away. I feel I always have to have the cell phone on. I don't want to miss anything. It's an ongoing distraction." Sound familiar?

I asked if he wanted to do something about his distractions so he would be able to focus and get good grades. Erik replied, "I have too. I have no choice. If not, I'll flunk out of school this time. Like one of the messages I have to reply to coming in right this second is from the pretty blonde I met last night at a party who wants to spend the day with me hiking. I have so many school-related things to do, and it would put me further behind."

We began to address his issues. I had Erik call upon his imagination to help him with images. I lit up his central pathway several times with gold light while he focused on the emotional intensity of his scenario of anxiety associated with the drama of texting. He commented, "That feeling is gone. It's a zero. I am in total command!"

He immediately began suggesting he could turn off the 'vibrate' mode on his cell phone that distracts him in class and study hour. He then came up the idea of making a deal with his dad for getting straight A's. Suggestions from others do not work when a pattern is in control. When a pattern is destroyed, suggestions bubble up from within the person himself or herself.

A call three weeks later found Erik doing much better. "I don't talk with the blonde girls any more and I canceled all my lunch dates because I have a paper to do. My grades aren't all 'A's yet, but I'm moving in that direction." When asked how he was doing with text messaging, he said, "I cut down quite a bit. I turned my cell off this weekend, for the most part, as well."

Using social media *without awareness* weakens your ability to become present or aware, and limits your ability to focus. Consequently, the choices that you make are limited to those specified by the patterns and your ability to see other options is greatly diminished. The inability to see options results in traffic-accident fatalities, train wrecks, poor and repetitive relationship choices, failed relationships, poor job performance, unwise career, business and investment choices, and a susceptibility to manipulation.

Surfing Porn Addiction All Better
Today's technology is a two-edged sword. Sergio, a 37-year-old married man with three children, found himself overwhelmed by a huge cut in his

salary, and his son's cancer treatment that drained both his emotional and financial bank accounts. He developed an addiction of our times.

Sergio initially entered pornographic sites out of curiosity, but eventually it ended the covenant of trust between him and his wife. When his wife first learned about his behavior, it did not seem to really upset her until she found Sergio's not only being on porn sites more frequently, but also lying to her about having just been on one. Sergio found himself in an inner conflict of trying to stop his addiction because his occupation required working from his house on his computer. The growing addiction added to his feelings of guilt and anxiety, which caused him to spend more time on porn sites and thereby inadvertently strengthened the patterns. Talk about a conundrum!

His desire to end the vicious circle brought him to call me. We worked for one session, and his inner conflict ended. Months later in a conversation, he excitedly reported, "My entire mental process was tweaked by what we did some time ago. It's really changed. Surfing porn ended and the thoughts to do so were somehow erased!"

Although it would appear that identifying and deleting an unconscious pattern is a formidable task, we will show you how the use of Cynthia's imagination made the task easier than you *think*.

Enslaved by Emails All Better

Cynthia, age 30, had it with her new job and was on the verge of quitting. She anxiously requested my waiting to begin our session until she finished responding to emails that had arrived on her computer during the drive to my office. I agreed. She talked non-stop: "I'm not effective at work. I stare at my emails. I get immobilized. I feel a lot of pressure from my new job even though it pays top salary with the commissions I make. I quit cigarettes six months ago and now all I do is deal with the stress and pressure. I feel like I'm in my own way. I'm so disorganized. I have a emails to respond to, and I foolishly avoid the most important top thirty of them and only respond to the most unimportant bottom thirty emails first because they're a 'no brainer' to do. I know I shouldn't. Then I feel guiltily and stressed, and I light up a cigarette again. I keep getting behind. I can't break this pattern."

I told her to slow down, take a breath, and we would get started. The work began when I asked her how she would like to feel if she were on top of her emails, completing the most important ones right away. The following is our dialogue:

"I'd feel calm. Focused. I need a block of time and not be enslaved by emails."

"Ask your imagination, and not yourself, to give you an image, person, cartoon, monster, object, etc. that makes you feel so stressed, pressured and anxious?"

"It's a kitchen timer."

"Ask the kitchen timer what its intention is to make you feel so stressed and anxious?"

"That's weird. It's smiling back at me now."

"Is it a smirky smile or a warm ingratiating one?"

"Kind of endearing."

"Good. That shows it's here to be of service to you. Tell that image to transform itself into the most positive image with the most positive energy that can help you feel relaxed and focused again."

"It's the same image of the kitchen timer, but the timer is now turned to one hour."

"Ask the kitchen timer if it is here to help you find a block of time so you can feel relaxed and focused and be able to handle whatever comes up."

"It becomes bigger now."

"How do you feel looking at the bigger image?"

"Calm. Doesn't make sense, but I feel very calm."

"Great. Embrace that image to come inside your heart, spirit and every cell in your body."

"It went right inside me."

"Now on a zero-to-10 scale, how high is the number associated with all the stress you were describing when you arrived here today?"

"Umm. I don't know. I can't locate any."
"What number is it?
"Has to be a zero. I can't feel anything but calmness."
I lit up Cynthia's central pathway to underscore the work we just did.

Five days later, Cynthia emailed me. "I am SO much better. I absolutely feel a major difference. I am doing tasks as they come in, instead of putting them off and procrastinating. I feel much more on top of everything and far less intimidated by my responsibilities. I still have a pile of old things to tackle, but not much new has been added. Work has been great. Still smoking ciggies, but I just *think* I'm not ready to quit that yet."

Notice how the pattern associated with her smoking just tricked her into believing it was *her* choice not to stop yet when she told me, "I just *think* I'm not ready to quit that yet." The pattern infiltrated her thoughts and made her rationalize her addiction to continue smoking. That is why a pattern is called a trickster. *Thinking*, "Should I, shouldn't I quit smoking?" only strengthens the pattern. Destroy the pattern before it destroys you.

Patterns and Privacy

People regularly post highly personal information, images and videos of themselves on the Internet, which cause some of them acute embarrassment, job losses, canceled employment offers, relationship breakups, barriers to promotion, loan denials, libel lawsuits, convictions for possessing child pornography and registration as sex offenders and other major lifetime annoyances. Does anyone actually volunteer for such serious consequences? Of course not. Then what motivates people to provide the entire world with a lifetime supply of rocks, over-ripe vegetables and even less wholesome substances to throw at them for the remainder of their lives? That motivation comes from the patterns within them, patterns that feed on the upsetting emotions of regret, fear, anger, worry, sadness, self-pity, grief, etc.

The Internet and the social media that it supports allow the patterns within us to be reinforced far more quickly than ever before. Like bloodhounds on the scent of seemingly elusive fugitive, patterns will use your use of social media to stir up more trouble than was ever possible before the Internet and social media existed. Like the unconscious that forever holds memories of everything you ever experienced, the Internet forever holds whatever highly personal information, images and videos that you post on a social media site or send via email.

There are businesses that offer to minimize the negative information that people post on the Internet. However, the businesses cannot erase the information. They create positive or neutral references on many web sites that they own. Search engines are then more likely to list the non-negative information on the first page or two of a query. The objective is to 'bury' the damaging information beneath pages of search results. The process is the electronic equivalent of burying a feeling under layers of other things to do and think about, which is fine if you can just not think about hamsters riding motorcycles. All the while, the damaging information remains sitting on a computer or server somewhere, vibrating with the frequency of the pattern that created it.

However, if the patterns that caused the posting of damaging information are not destroyed, then the damaging information will surely surface at some time, drawn to the pattern that created it like an iron filing to a magnet. The only solution to being free from the threat of the damaging information is the destruction of the patterns that feed from your upsetting emotions attached to that information. Destroying those patterns removes the attraction between you and that information. Like your memory that no longer has an attached, upsetting emotion after a pattern is destroyed, the information on the Internet can never cause you harm after the patterns that created it are destroyed.

Identifying repeating or upsetting situations in your life and destroying the patterns behind them is the ounce of prevention that is worth far, far more than the pound of cure after the fact. Destroying the patterns within you will give you the freedom and power that being present to what is happening in the moment is all about. You, and not a pattern, are then in control of *your* choices, which will be proper for you and those affected by your choices. With the patterns and their insatiable needs for your upsetting emotions annihilated, you cannot be set up for the current and long-lasting misery that they feed upon.

It Chooses, Not You

You never question the nature of what you are experiencing because you identify so closely with the operations of a pattern, you assume that if you do something better, quicker, more cleverly or smarter, then you will experience a more satisfactory outcome. When the result still does not meet your expectations, you may get angry and blame yourself and then do the task just a bit differently. However, because your actions have been determined by the pattern, the next result will also usually be unsatisfactory and your upsetting emotional reactions will only serve to strengthen the pattern's cunning operations.

For example, people who as children rarely received their parents' approval will continuously seek that approval from adults, but they will seek the approval from those who cannot or will not give it. Persons who are seeking approval dictated by the pattern will find themselves in work and social situations where approval will never be given, and the pattern will be strengthened even further. Like a stage hypnotist who makes audience members *bark like a dog*, a pattern makes you see things and feel the way it chooses, not you.

Imagine All Better offers you freedom.

15

Free Will, Free Choice and Patterns

> *"... we too easily assume that we are our real selves, and that our choices are really the ones we want to make when, in fact, our acts of free choice are (though morally imputable, no doubt) largely dictated by psychological compulsions, flowing from our inordinate ideas of our own importance. Our choices are too often dictated by our false selves."*
>
> — Thomas Merton, Theologian and Trappist monk

WE NAIVELY BELIEVE that we are the superior ones in control of our lives at all times with our great intellectual understanding. We deal with our environment according to our interpretation of what we have observed or experienced in the past. Your interpretations of your past observations and experiences are determined by patterns. Every single moment is unique; no moment can be duplicated. However, you assume that every situation you encounter is just like some other situation that came before it, and the choice you made then will work just as well now. Your assumption that you can analyze all potential options and choose an effective action in the current moment is also an illusion. Patterns mechanistically make you react automatically in each moment and make you remain unaware of the limits on your perceptions, reactions and choices.

Until a pattern is destroyed, your perceptions and interpretations of your environment will be determined by the pattern's operation. It is as if an invisible opponent has taken total control your freedom – your free will and free choice. Until you destroy the patterns that are causing your difficulty, your choices will be limited to those choices that are within the patterns' realm of operation to maintain their survival. What you call free will or free choice is an illusion because your choices are governed by patterns' operations, which have only their survival as their sole operating principle.

The concept of free will or free choice implies that you have awareness of all available options and total control over which option you choose. However, patterns, and not you, make you believe that you are aware of all the effective available options. A pattern will give you tunnel vision and allow you to see only those options that are non-threatening to the sinister pattern's existence and enhance the pattern's survival. If you had free will or free choice, then you could will or choose to perceive the situation in a different fashion whenever you wanted. If you had free will and free choice, you could easily change your emotion to any emotion you wanted by changing your thoughts about your situation. However, you have *no* control over your thoughts. In order to prove this seemingly wild, blasphemous statement to yourself, do the following five-minute exercise:

Sit quietly observing your mind for five minutes with your eyes open or closed. You will find that you cannot control or stop your thinking because the mind produces thoughts the way the body produces perspiration. Also pay attention to your thoughts during the day or when you awaken in the middle of the night. They will go non-stop often with negative, worrisome themes such as what you coulda, woulda, shoulda, oughta have said or done in situations that day.

When we propose there is no such thing as free will and choice in our lives, we are referring to situations where a pattern is operating that makes *all* of us believe whatever we do or say is our choice and comes from our free will, when indeed it does not. Since nothing in the environment has an emotion attached to it, any discomfort with what you are reading here is coming from within you. Specifically, patterns within you are causing those feelings. Patterns cause you to feel justified about your beliefs, emotions, actions and words. Patterns have prevented mankind from learning from its mistakes and keep us repeating the same "choices" and behaviors. This is why history repeats itself over and over. Our wars, murders, physical and emotional abuse, suicides, betrayals, genocide and religious persecution will continue until our patterns are acknowledged and destroyed.

Classic examples are New Year's resolutions like losing weight, cutting back or eliminating cigarettes or alcohol, overcoming the anxiety of flying or speaking in public. You need to open your eyes wide to the patterns that have you under their control in these situations. A pattern will yank you, like a dog on a leash, whenever you get close to reaching your goals, or *think* you have reached them. This is why star athletes suddenly lose their amazing skills. This is why men and women get into dead-end relationships again and again. This is why addicts in rehab programs usually require several passes through the program before they achieve recovery, if ever. This is why obese individuals who undergo dramatic weight loss will generally regain the weight, and then some. This is why people who have substance abuse issues will usually have many relapses while they work on becoming clean. This is why career criminals commit serial crimes over many years and chronically enter and leave prisons. In these cases, the patterns within these people remain undetected and grow stronger throughout time. Eventually, either the people with the patterns die with the patterns or the patterns become so strong that they kill the people who host them through alcohol, drugs or personal neglect. For these people, life is miserable, and they know it, but they feel powerless to change. For these people, searching for the reason *why* they behave the way they do will only strengthen the patterns. You can expect freedom only after you destroy a pattern with the Imagine All Better process.

Imagine All Better allows you to quickly and easily destroy the patterns that separate you from your free will and free choice and prevent you from seeing a wider selection of more powerful options due to the patterns' intrusiveness. Like many other areas of your life, you must have the experience in order to understand and accept the power of your imagination and the ease with which you can destroy patterns. The reward for doing so is the inner peace that you have read about in any places, but have never experienced.

In summary, you are living your life like a guitar in its well-fitting case where only a tiny amount of wiggle room is available. The patterns constructs and maintains the case you are in, but the little wiggle room, which is the conscious awareness that you have, is more than enough to allow you to destroy the case. All the analysis in the world cannot get out of the case you are confined to; you can only Imagine All Better.

Getting off the Patterns' Coins

You *assume* that making a choice that is different from, or perhaps opposite to, a choice that you normally make is an example of free will or free choice. However, such choices are based upon your normal reaction, which means that you are being directed by the result of the pattern's influence. For example, if you are a high-risk-taking investor, then choosing a safe, low-risk investment as a means to counteract the pattern's influence is not a free choice. This is because the effects of the pattern on your perception motivate your choice of the safer investment. The 'choices' are mechanized by the patterns' operation, not your desires.

In other words, you have merely moved along the spectrum from the riskier to the safer investment, but the influence of the pattern is still there. Your choices that are motivated by the pattern's need for negative emotional energy will strengthen the pattern. A pattern has only its survival as its goal; it does not place any value on you. Like a flea or a tick that you pick up while hiking in the woods, a pattern is unconcerned with your well-being. Because a pattern cannot think, it is not plotting to be your enemy; it is merely operating automatically during every moment. But you mistake the pattern as being yourself, which causes you to mistakenly conclude that, "I sabotage myself; I am my worst enemy."

Another example is that of a violent criminal who becomes a religious believer while in prison, but his change may be one of degree and not of substance. His conversion moved him from one side of a coin to the other side, but it is still the same coin.

People who attend numerous workshops in the pursuit of a spiritual answer need to examine their motivation for attending the workshops. You may attend a workshop to seek a higher level of awareness, but the higher awareness state represents the other side of the coin. The pattern will cause you to feel that there is always something missing and will cause you to continue to seek without end. Unless you destroy the pattern, you will always feel that the awareness you seek is beyond your grasp. Therefore, you will always have feelings of frustration, incompleteness and dissatisfaction. Destroying the pattern that motivates you to seek answers *outside* yourself will allow you to remove the clutter in your mind that prevents you from getting a clear picture of what you are truly seeking. Until you examine *your* intentions that produce repetitive frustrating results, the pattern will continue to operate. The price tag is dear for all the emotions a pattern stirs up to camouflage its operations, and you are left to blame yourself as the culprit, the saboteur and creator of all your terrible choices.

Your tasks are to become aware that there is a coin, and then to remove yourself from the coin by destroying the patterns that cause you difficulty. Once those patterns are destroyed, they can never be reconstructed because the patterns formed at a unique moment in time can never be duplicated. Just as you will find yourself in a unique moment when you finish reading this sentence, returning to read the beginning of the same sentence is another unique moment. A pattern that you just destroyed can never be reactivated, because your expanded awareness will prevent it from being reinstalled. You cannot get on the same subway car with the same people ever again; you cannot put your foot in the same river twice; you can never go home again; and you can *never* be reinfected with the same pattern.

In addition, the energy that the pattern stole from you is now available to you in the form of awareness, meaning knowing what is happening in the moment, which means that you can now turn that awareness onto other patterns in your life and begin to destroy them as well. And when the patterns are destroyed, you have a better chance to access your right-brain wisdom, knowing without thinking, and your unlimited creative capability. The reward for destroying patterns is that your choices will include unobstructed access the wisdom of the collective unconscious. You will know without thinking what your most effective choice is, just like you know without thinking what you want to eat from a menu selection just by reading descriptions of a fillet mignon, grilled salmon or that incredible hot fudge sundae.

When you destroy the patterns that are associated with your stories, you no longer have the compulsion to act out those stories in order to generate their associated emotions. This allows you to be in the here and now, to choose an action or words that fit the situation. And when you no longer identify with the emotions tied to your story, especially a story that causes you pain or anger, you have forgiven all those involved in the story – including yourself. You have the freedom to move on with your life, unaffected by the negative feelings that have troubled you.

Social Anxiety and Panic Attacks All Better

Margaret was about to turn 30. She had been struggling mightily with medical problems and depression for several years and was unable to hold a job. She called me because a pattern in her, had painted her into a corner of anxiety that isolated her socially. Margaret said, "I have social anxiety. I don't go out of my apartment. Even the *thought* of going out gives me a panic attack. My anxiety has been building up. It's different from real depression, but similar in some ways. Hard to explain. My whole body and head tell me that I can't do it. Can't go out! My fear is I'll have to talk with people. My 30th birthday is next month, and I have always wanted to have a party to celebrate it. But I get more panicky as my birthday approaches because it means socializing."

A few weeks later following two session with her, we spoke again. Margaret reported her social anxiety no longer controlled her. She said, "I'm signing up for a painting class tonight. Actually, I'm picking up somebody tonight for a friend at the airport. I've never met this woman before, and I'm not anxious. So I guess the social anxiety is gone! Remember my friend I avoided talking with at a coffee shop a couple of weeks ago, and I snuck out before she saw me? Well, I'm no longer avoiding her, or anybody."

Two weeks later, Margaret reported that she was feeling much better and had successfully celebrated her birthday party with friends. Will she need to continue working on patterns? Absolutely. As you continue to destroy your patterns, you will become aware of other patterns operating. Trying to understand patterns wins you the booby prize; annihilating patterns wins you freedom.

Imagine All Better offers you freedom.

Section Three

What You Need to Destroy Patterns

"If a teacher is indeed wise
He does not bid you enter
The house of his wisdom,
But rather leads you to the
Threshold or your own mind."

— Kahlil Gibran

16

Patterns Use Your Discomfort

"We have accepted separative concepts based on sense impressions as the final reality for so long that the boundaries they reflect have established themselves inviolable. We respond to them as we do to the mime who makes us believe in an invisible wall which he creates with his gestures. We then limit ourselves to conform to the wall which we imagine to be there."

— SHIRLEY NICHOLSON

A PATTERN EXPERTLY USES your awareness of disturbing emotions to hide behind. When your attention begins to approach a pattern, the pattern keeps you from getting any closer by generating upsetting, unpleasant emotions and feelings. A pattern uses an associated memory to cloak itself. For example, if you have a conversation and hear a critical word or see a stern facial expression that goes back to a perceived upsetting experience involving an authority figure, then feelings of low self-esteem and ridicule will be triggered within you. The emotions associated with those distant events are so minute that you are never conscious of them.

And if you persevere with an intention to destroy the button-pushing, crazy-making pattern, then the pattern will fight desperately for its existence like a wild animal saving its life. Stronger and stronger upsetting feelings will overwhelm you and become the focus of your attention. You will avoid these feelings by staying away from the pattern. You will notice heavy feelings in your stomach, chest or back, accompanied by feelings of procrastination, denial, anger or depression. You will lose your intention to go near any pattern in the future in order to avoid such agonizing discomfort.

Do not expect to find emotional relief from telling your, 'You-won't-believe-what-happened-to-me-again' story to a friend, or even a bartender. Why? Because the pattern is still intact, and an hour later, you will still feel the same upsetting emotions. Furthermore, looking *outside* yourself for relief from your emotions of rejection, fear, or never feeling good enough will never prove satisfactory. The pattern will allow you to see only those situations that do not threaten the pattern. You must destroy the pattern to find relief. Your desire to be free is what gives you the motivation to read this book and use the approach described here. You have the option to use the Imagine All Better app on your smartphone, tablet or computer to walk you through the process from beginning to end.

You cannot use intellectual, rational methods to analyze or control patterns. A pattern exists in the unconscious, while the analytical intellect exists only in the conscious. You cannot know the extent of the unconscious, since, by definition, it contains all those processes, feelings, emotions, impressions, hunches and insights that exist outside your present awareness. Unconscious processes control not only your bodily functions such as circulation, breathing, digestion and immune responses, but also how and what you perceive in each moment. A pattern can never be defeated by logic because patterns dominate your thoughts, analyses and rationalizations. You must enter the patterns' invisible world by using your imagination that can make the invisible, visible, in the blink of an eye, where you can confront and destroy patterns.

What Will Work

The key idea here is that nothing, or 'no thing', can be 'done', which is where observation, or awareness, a 'non-doing' state gives you the only tool needed to annihilate the pattern. You need only to 'not-do', to be, in order to be successful in eliminating a pattern. The instant that you begin to 'do', think, say or act in order to destroy a pattern, you are back in your analytical brain, which is incapable of destroying the pattern. You need only to observe, without thinking, what is happening in the moment, which includes what you observe in your imagination.

Observation does not involve 'doing'. Quantum mechanics has shown that whatever we observe, or focus our attention on, is altered. That is, both the observer and the subject are changed merely by observing the subject. For example, when you have a telephone conversation, your words change something within the person with whom you are speaking, and the person's words, which have been influenced by your words, will change something within you. Since all 'doing' about destroying a pattern is motivated by the pattern itself, there is nothing that you can 'do' to get rid of it.

When a detrimental pattern is obliterated, you can recognize other potential options that were always present, but were obscured by the pattern's operation. This allows you to see alternative choices in a particular situation and thereby allows you to make an effective choice, one that benefits you, and not the pattern. By now, you understand that in order to destroy a pattern, there is nothing, 'no thing' to do, 'no thing' to get, and 'no where' to go. You are already where you need to be, in the right place. You need only to observe what is going on in the moment. Your observation is all that you need, and you have that capability in its full measure right now. You have always had it, and always will.

A pattern was your invisible internal opponent, a parasitical virus, until now. And like a parasite, a pattern infected and possessed your mind, thoughts, feelings, attitudes, and perceptions. You wound up doing its bidding and not that which brought you harmony and balance. This energy-sucking virus disconnected you from the balancing energies that can ensure your peace of mind, optimism, enthusiasm, self-confidence and joy. Patterns caused the continuous disconnections that eventually resulted in a domino effect compromising your medical, emotional and spiritual well being. As this fissure between you widened, the patterns became stronger by siphoning your energy. The wider this abyss, the more vulnerable you were to depressions, anxieties, addictions, broken relationships, medical symptoms, chronic pains, and even suicide and homicide.

You now understand the nature and operation of patterns. You are now aware of how they have directed your life. Your current awareness by itself is the crucial first step in the process of annihilating the patterns that have robbed you of the full enjoyment of your life. Your awareness guarantees that the patterns can no longer operate without interference.

What Won't Work

Avoiding or dismissing thoughts about an unpleasant situation, such as filing your income tax return, going to a dentist or ending a relationship, *appears* to produce relief from the negative feelings, but the pattern's existence is left intact when you do so. Unfortunately, avoiding thoughts is much like the statement, "Don't think about pink elephants." Therefore, looking the other way generates and enhances background noises of worrisome inner chatter. Your disturbing scenario plays continuously *along with* your associated upsetting emotions much to your exasperation. Your avoidance now takes the form of talking incessantly, using the Internet, alcohol, drugs, texting, food, cooking, shopping, workaholism, or any all-consuming activity to drown out the background unpleasantness. You can also become depressed or angry with yourself when your efforts fail.

Income Tax Procrastination All Better

Thomas, age 45, called me a week before his final extension was due to file his income tax. Thomas was in a 'Catch-22' scenario. If he did not submit his taxes now, he feared he would be in serious trouble with the Internal Revenue Service. He postponed it until the last possible moment because he would become anxious and depressed simply "thinking" about how bad the previous year had been financially. Thinking is neither good nor bad, unless it goes through a pattern's filter and your perception of your thoughts are emotionally charged.

Was Thomas responsible for creating his current dilemma? Of course not, the anxiety was being amplified by - you guessed it - the pattern! See how you are beginning to spot it? The pattern's intention is to make you believe that you are creating all your unwanted issues and emotions in your life. Here is how the conversation went with Thomas:

"I don't like *its* pulling me into an area of anxiety and depression and being mad at myself."

"How does doing your taxes overwhelm you?"

"It's whenever I begin to view the paperwork of my losses and gains in stocks. Those losses killed me last year. I knew it was bad, but not *that* bad. I can't get those numbers out of my head....the damage I did financially."

"OK. Let's go. On a zero-to-10 scale, how high is the intensity of your emotions of being mad your yourself, anxious and depressed whenever you remember those bad loses?"

"It's a ten."

"Hold onto that memory in your mind while I keep lighting up your central pathway with gold light to see if the numbers drop. What number is it now?"

"It's a nine."

"And now?"

"It's a four.

It then dropped to a two, a one, and then to a zero. "Now try very hard to bring back the feelings of anxiety, depression and being angry off at yourself."

"I can't. There seems to be a disconnection. I'm not seeing those stock figures in as much detail in my mind now. The numbers that were in red on the paperwork are now grayish. I'm not pleased with what happened, but no more resentment and being mad at myself is left. I'm not picking up those feelings any more."

You will notice whenever a pattern is unknowingly being made reference to, many times the pattern is labeled as "it", "its" or "something" that is causing the perplexing emotions. In Thomas' case, he believed he was referencing the issue of doing his income taxes, yet you can observe the pattern's operation in Thomas' opening comment above: "I don't like *its* pulling me into an area of anxiety and depression and being mad at myself."

Thomas called me a few days later on his way home from his accountant's office just in time to avoid a penalty. He told me he was "a happy camper and totally relieved."

A pattern thus defends itself from your awareness by causing you to "do something" about the unpleasant emotions caused by its operation. Doing something will always fail, of course, because the pattern can never be satisfied and *it* permits you, like a prison guard would, to do *only* those things that do not threaten its existence. A pattern's demands for your upsetting emotional energy cannot and will never be satisfied because it never matures, it never stops growing, and it never dies on its own.

Patterns are responsible for your perceptions, what you have come to believe as your "reality", because they permit you to see only those things that do not threaten their existences. In fact, you are not your patterns. Patterns do not serve you. They are energetic parasites that rely on your painful emotions of worry, anger, despair, etc. for their continued existence. Unless a pattern is destroyed, it will continue to dictate your life and cause you to experience a repetitious, familiar sequence of disturbing circumstances. So, if you find yourself asking questions such as, "How do I get myself into these situations again?" or "How come I'm so unlucky?" or "Why do I always find losers?" - begin to look for patterns. Patterns, not you, got you there – and will get you there again and again and again and again until you destroy them.

Take a good look at your own life and that of your parents, grandparents, siblings, friends, people you stopped dating, former friends you never speak to again, quirky bosses, sports figures, celebrities, etc. Can you identify patterns that had or still do run you or others? Things that you or they struggle with are patterns. Things or behaviors you cannot overcome and give into are patterns. While watching TV dramas, sitcoms, movies, the news, etc., you will see how patterns are in control, running the show. Everybody worldwide has patterns controlling him or her. Everybody has the capability of destroying patterns. You have patterns running you. The contents of this book give you the capability to destroy any pattern. If you doubt you can, then that may be the first pattern for you to address and annihilate – it is easier than you <u>think</u>!

You are now beginning to understand the nature and operation of patterns and how they have controlled your life. Your current awareness by itself is the crucial first step to annihilating patterns that have robbed you of the full enjoyment of your life. Your awareness of patterns' existences is critical in being able to identify and destroy them. The importance of destroying a detrimental pattern cannot be over emphasized. Obliterating a pattern enhances your ability to destroy other patterns and reclaim your energy that was feeding the patterns.

Imagine All Better offers you freedom.

17

An Overview of How to Destroy Patterns

"Positive images of the future are a powerful and magnetic force...They draw us on and energize us, give us courage and will to take important initiatives. Negative images of the future also have magnetism. They pull the spirit downward in the path of despair."

— WILLIAM JAMES, FATHER OF AMERICAN PSYCHOLOGY

THE FOLLOWING PARAGRAPHS are an overview of how to destroy a pattern, which is an organized invisible energy that exists in your unconscious. This may seem like an impossible task since patterns control your perceptions, thoughts and feelings and therefore, will not permit themselves to be annihilated. Patterns' invisibility and their use of every bit of highly personal knowledge about you to cause you to be distracted through rationalizations and great emotional discomfort adds to the problem of destroying the pattern. So, what to do?

The answer to how to destroy patterns is simple – Don't think about it. The answer is don't think about it? Yes! Since patterns control your thoughts and thinking cannot work, then don't think! How do you *not* think? You are not thinking when you observe a sunset, a baby smiling, the first flowers of spring or are simply tossing a wad of crumpled paper into a trash basket.

Here is an example of an activity you do every day that makes use of the elements that you need to destroy a pattern – and you perform these elements perfectly now! This demonstration contains the three elements necessary for destroying patterns: intention, attention and detachment.

A Really Simple Demonstration

Hold a small object, such as a pen or a coin, between your thumb and forefinger. Put your other hand beneath the object and when you are ready, release your hold on the object. Observe carefully what is happening in your mind during this simple exercise. Repeat this exercise several times, taking great care to watch the sequence of events that lead up to and follow your release of the object.

What This Really Simple Demonstration Shows You

First, ask yourself the question: "Why did I release my hold on the item?" You might respond: "Because you told me to let go of the object." But why did you choose that particular moment to release your hold on the object? You would probably reply: "Because I wanted to." You form an intention to release the object, and that intention led you to open your fingers. So, you understand from this exercise that *intention* precedes action, thought and behavior.

While you were looking at your hand and the object, you were probably not thinking. You were curious about what you were supposed to observe. During this period of no thought, your brain was in the alpha brain-wave state. That is, your brain-wave frequency was about seven or eight cycles per second, which is much less than the beta-wave state of 15 to 30 cycles per second. The beta-wave state is the state that you are in when you are thinking or speaking. In order to perform energy balancing successfully, you must be in the alpha brain-wave state, which is easily entered.

Finally, once you released your hold on the object, it fell. Your control of the object ended, and its path was fixed by gravity. Despite your thoughts, emotions and body movements, the object's path and its final resting place were beyond your influence and control at the instant of its release from your grip. Your acceptance of this fact is called detachment. Detachment means that you care about the outcome, but you also understand that the outcome is beyond your control, and that you will accept the result without judgment. Remember, once you speak your words or complete your action, you have no control over how they will be perceived. The consequences of your words or action are another matter entirely; the perception of your words or actions are in the recipient's control, not yours.

There you have the three necessary elements that you need to destroy patterns – intention, attention and detachment. We will describe in greater detail each of the elements' use in destroying patterns in Section Four.

I remember being invited to a New Years' Eve party and was unable to find a parking space for at least eight blocks in either direction. The only 'parking space' I noticed was across the street from the party, but I would be blocking the crosswalk, not the best choice. So I reflected on parking there only after I detached from the outcome of getting a parking ticket as I would be willing to pay the price of the ticket for such a great space. I had an ear-to-ear grin on my face when I left the party at 3 a.m. and found my car still there, and no ticket!

Imagine All Better offers you freedom.

Section Four

How to Destroy Patterns

"Healing does not come from increasing the amount of light in our lives, but rather from reaching into the shadow and drawing up unreconciled elements of ourselves into the light where they can be healed."

— Tao-te-Ching

18

How to Destroy Patterns

"The new reality ushered in by quantum physics is possible for the first time to manipulate the invisible intelligence that underlies the visible world. Einstein taught us that the physical body, like all material objects is an illusion and trying to manipulate it can be like grasping the shadow and missing the substance. The unseen world is the real world, and when we are willing to explore the unseen levels...we can tap in to the immense creative power that lies at our source."

— Deepak Chopra

Until now, you probably felt that your life was determined by random events that usually produced fearful and worrisome emotions along with the occasional happy ones. Most sources give instructions for putting bandaids on your emotional wounds and hoping for the best, but now you know you can go well beyond this practice. You have within you an infinitely powerful capability that not only heals the wounds and removes the bandaids, but also makes you wound- proof and removes all traumas from those wounds. You may feel that the world is increasingly dysfunctional, that you're a complex person and your problems are hopeless, but you will soon learn a method that will keep you balanced and centered in the middle of any emotional storm you may encounter. You are more powerful than you have ever guessed, because you control your imagination whose power has no limitations.

As you remove your patterns, your detrimental attachment to certain people, activities, ideas, beliefs and objects disappears. In place of attachment, you will find detachment, which is your enjoyment of whatever you are doing or experiencing, but with the understanding that these things cannot bring you a sense of completion or balance. You are complete as you are. There is nothing outside of yourself that is necessary to complete you. And so you will become detached and free, enjoying your life while knowing without thinking that nothing outside yourself can bring you lasting satisfaction.

A friend of mine for twenty years was diagnosed with ovarian cancer. Gail appeared younger than her stated age of 50 and was a teacher of children with special needs. She was health conscious, exercised daily, read ferociously, and even participated weekly in an all-male drumming group. She handled her diagnosis with an incredible determination to overcome it, until she read a popular book that stated if you have her type of cancer that you also had a certain percentage of developing other cancers in the future. That broke her resolve, and she called me at my office crying uncontrollably. I had her come by and bring that book. I walked her through the landscape of her imagination with Imagine All Better, and her fear and depression vanished instantaneously; she felt empowered and was laughing as she left my office. A pattern that attached anxiety and fear to the content of that book was triggered, and was now destroyed. I told her to burn the book when she got home. Thirteen years later, she is still symptom free and continues to walk every year in the Prevent Ovarian Cancer 6K fundraiser.

We will now present you with a detailed description of how to destroy patterns. The following overview will guide you an understanding the Imagine All Better process and how to use it on family and friends, young and old, as well as your clients and patients. Appendix B contains some the many applications of our work to many professions. Since you have already become familiar with our approach through some of our case examples, it will make understanding this section a bit easier. Using Imagine All Better is like any other skill that you have learned and in time will become as easy as reading, making a pot of coffee or tea, or riding a bicycle.

There are four principal steps involved in destroying patterns:

-Telling the story,
-Rating the story's emotional intensity,
-Lighting up the person's central pathway, and
-Using the Imagination.

Step 1. Telling the 'Story':

Just about everyone wants to tell you their stories that contain patterns that obstruct them from reaching their hopes and dreams. Everyone likes to be heard and to feel that they matter. Your listening to their stories provides them with the acknowledgement, attention and affirmation that they seek.

Remember, the pattern is motivating them to tell the story, relive the emotions associated with it, and thereby reinforcing the pattern. So, once you have heard a minimal amount of information, kindly interrupt them for any more details. Just ask them what upsetting emotions are associated with their story, say sad or scared, and what those emotions would be when they are 'all better', say happy or relieved. Do not accept descriptions of all-better feelings such as "better", "okay", "stress-free", "great", etc. That is all you need: the emotions connected with the problem and with the problem all better.

Actually, you can use the Imagine All Better approach without having to hear any part of their story whatsoever. This shortcut allows their right to privacy as the story may be too embarrassing, painful or shameful to share, especially if they are a family member or close friend. This approach allows anyone to resolve guarded events in their lives that they otherwise would have taken to their graves before ever sharing with another soul.

You will occasionally encounter people's stories that will remain unaffected by your application of Imagine All Better. Over time, some people come to completely identify with their stories of say, 'victimization' or 'never getting a break in life', and their stories become embedded themes for how they identify themselves, how their egos present themselves to the world. After they have acted in the starring roles in their stories' scripts for a sufficiently long time, it becomes very difficult, if not impossible, to break their hold on their story or - the hold the story has on them. The patterns have become deeply entrenched, taken over completely and will use the persons' fear or determination to make them defend themselves. Usually, the patterns will convince them that they and the patterns are really one and the same, and if they let go of their programmed, hypnotic, repetitive, never-ending story, then they will no longer exist and will vanish into nothingness along with their story. These people will continue to live their painful narratives proudly despite your efforts.

When you encounter situations in which people cling desperately to their story, remember to remain detached as if you were objectively observing their stories of 'life's unfair', 'nothing good ever happens to me', or 'why is everybody else happy/prosperous/in love and I'm not'? The patterns in you will interact with the patterns in everyone around you. So detachment will prevent your emotions such as frustration, anger, despair, worry, sadness, pity, condemnation, superiority, etc. from feeding the patterns within them and the patterns within you.

Step 2. Rating the Story's Emotional Intensity:
The emotions associated with a story may be a specific emotion or a combination of worry, anger, doubt, frustration, fear, etc. – an emotional 'soup' of different emotions. It is important that people are able to rate

the intensity of the emotions connected with their story on a numerical scale. A zero-to-10 numerical scale serves quite well for them to assign a number to their intense feelings associated with their story. Zero represents the all-better emotions that they would like to have such as happiness, contentment, freedom, etc., and the numbers between one and 10 represent the degrees of intensity of their upsetting emotions of fear, sadness, anger, etc. Using a subjective rating scale allows both of you to determine the presence and intensity of a pattern.

Sometimes people will rank the numerical scale using a combination of numbers that works just as well. For example, they may say, "It's a 7 or 8" or "a 3 or a 4." Other times people will state that they are unable to supply a numerical rating, particularly if they have never been asked to do it before. In those cases, just ask them to make up a number. Remember, there are no 'right' or 'wrong', 'good' or 'bad' answers.

In some cases, people may rank the associated emotions at some number greater than 10. Since you are interested in a measure of emotional intensity, some number greater than 10 is acceptable for your purposes, and you would begin with that number. In other cases, children may be able to rank the emotional intensity easier on a tiny-to-huge scale, which is also useful for gauging emotional intensity. Whatever the scale chosen, the objective is to assess the intensity of the associated emotions and the effect of your work on that intensity.

Out of the Ashes and All Better

Juel, age 37, was referred by her naturopath whom I had worked with in the past. When I asked Juel what she wanted to work on, an immediate deep sigh came from her, followed by silence. The previous year her house, where she conducted her practiced as a physical therapist, burned to the ground. I asked Juel to select a specific memory associated with her loss and rate the intensity of her "sadness and grief" for the loss of her house on a zero-to-10 scale. She estimated it to be an eight or nine.

I lit up her central pathway with gold light from the bridge of her nose to tip of her tailbone. I would do that each time she reported the numbers dropping. If she reported the numbers going all the way down to zero and that feeling could not be retrieved again, the process would be completed. However, if the numbers she reported became stuck at a particular number, and/or moved higher on the scale, I would then work with her imagination and afterward return to her evaluating the zero-to-10 numbers until they were a zero.

Juel reported the intensity of her sadness dropping to a four or five, then a two or three and it would not moved past a two no matter how many times I would light up her central pathway. Her imagination was called upon to give her an image associated with her sadness and grief and it produced what she described as "a big scary monster hovering over my back and enveloping my back", who told her its intention was for her "to feel pain". I told her to imagine herself 50 or 100 times bigger than the monster. Since the monster's response represented one of ten worldwide patterns called a 'parasite' that lived off of her being in pain, she destroyed it by freezing it and broke it into little chips.

She then said if her grief and deep sadness were all better, she would "feel light and open". Her imagination complied by presenting her with a positive image of a blue sky with clouds that symbolized her feeling light and open again. However, when asked to see if there was a skeptic for that image, she agreed. Her imagination gave her the image of an ex-boyfriend whose purpose was "to control me". Power and/or Control are also one of the 10 universal patterns. When instructed to annihilate his image, she said, "He's burned to ashes. I imagined using fire from the sun to burn him." Her imagination replaced him immediately with an image of pure bright sunshine rays that make her feel light and open again.

I had her return to the original upsetting scenario and rank her feelings of being uncomfortable and sad on the zero-to-10 scale where zero was her being very open, light, relaxed and at peace. Juel reported its being a zero and her previous upsetting emotions were completely gone and her feeling open and light were back.

Step 3. Lighting Up the Person's Central Pathway:

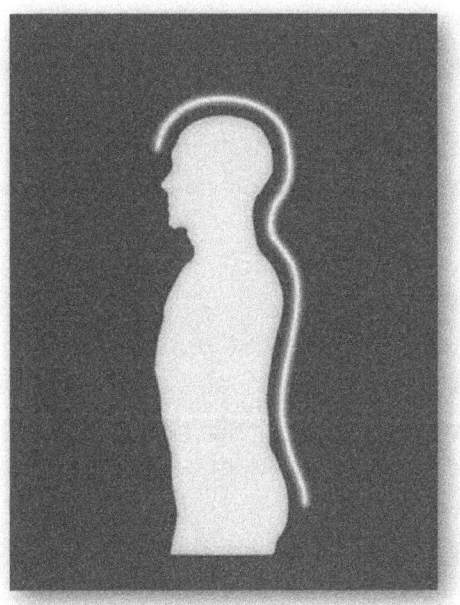

Lighting up the Central Pathway

Lighting up the central pathway removes emotions generated by patterns that have become stuck somewhere in the person's energy field and thereby blocks the normal flow of energy and vitality. This blockage can result in feeling emotionally overloaded, feeling low energy, presenting physical symptoms and depressing the immune system. Imagine if your kitchen sink were backed up because something had gotten blocked in the pipe. Upon removing it, the water would flow, and you would have full access to the use of your sink again.

It is not important to know exactly where the particular upsetting emotions are located in the body. Why? Because all energy pathways in the body feed off the spinal column. You can light up the central pathway by using your imagination to apply gold light to it. The central pathway is a line that begins on the bridge of the nose, between the center of the eyebrows, extends over the top of the head and down the spinal column to the tip of the tailbone. In the same way you can imagine a purple elephant turning into a gold elephant, you can easily imagine the central pathway being lit up with gold light. Imagine applying gold light with a paintbrush, a 'magic wand', a flashlight projecting gold light, a mirror reflecting golden sunlight, turning on a master light switch, or any method that you feel comfortable with using. Or simply imagine gold light illuminating from the bridge of your nose to the tip of your tailbone.

In this manner, you can remove any distressing associated emotions from the person. In addition, you will apply intention, attention, and detachment that you learned in the preceding pages. Here is how you do it:

Ask the people you are working with to assign a number from zero-to-10 that represents the intensity of the emotions associated with the story they wish to receive relief from. After forming an *intention* to bring balance to them, you would enter the alpha state of no thought. You need to remain detached from the outcome and any expectations on yourself to do well.

Your intention will take care of the necessary details, even if you have never met the people, or if they are on the other side of the Earth. Your intention to bring balance and enter an alpha state will automatically allow you to work with them. The alpha state occurs without thinking by focusing your attention on the spot where air enters your nostrils, and the spot where air exists your nostrils a few times while simultaneously, without thought, imagining gold light filling up the person's central pathway. You need not imagine a detailed image of them or their central pathways, something as simple as a crude figure in the drawing on the previous page will do nicely

Another way to quiet your thoughts for a second or two while focusing on your breathing would be to internally ask yourself one of the following three statements with no intention of expecting an answer: "Tell me something I don't know.", and be quiet. Or "Where will my next thought come from?", and be quiet. Or "I'm aware of being aware.", and be quiet.

IMAGINE ALL BETTER

Take a moment now and ask yourself either one of these statements and notice what happens. In the quiet space that follows, your mind is empty of thought for a few seconds so you can immediately perform your focused breathing exercise while imagining lighting up their central pathway. You need only to be in the "no-thought" space for a few seconds or less in order to be effective at lighting up the central pathway.

Sometimes a troublesome emotion will begin to drop in intensity from the highest number they report on the zero-to-10 scale to a zero rather quickly by lighting up their central pathway. And if you are like us when we first began lighting up the central pathway, you will also not believe what just happened! At times, it occurs that quickly. For example, if they report the number starting at an eight, you would have them focus on their original upsetting scenario with the intensity of an eight while you light up their central pathway. Then ask them, "What number is it now?" They may report it dropped to a five or a six. You would ask them to focus on their original scenario of the intensity of a five or six and light up their central pathway again. Each time they report a lower number you would repeat the same instructions and light up their central pathway until they report the number being a zero, and they can no longer bring the emotions of the scenario to mind no matter how hard they try - even if their lives depended upon it! We always light up the central pathway one more time for good measure. In these cases, you have permanently removed the troubling associated emotions, and you can move on to other issues that the person may wish to discuss.

However, always double-check by asking them if there is still a glimmer of an upsetting emotion, a tentacle of a feeling holding onto them, a thread of anxiety, discomfort, upset, etc. Have them shake the tree of emotions to see if any other upsetting emotions are still hanging on. Have them look at that upsetting memory again while you have them simultaneously repeat to themselves one of those three statements that will quiet their mind for a few seconds. That will quiet their mind from thinking for a few seconds to get an accurate feedback. If they do report a lingering emotion hanging on or a physical discomfort such as a stomach or chest sensation, you would have them rank the intensity of the lingering emotion or physical sensation. Start over again by lighting up their central pathway as they stay focused on the intensity of a number associated with the new feelings. When they cannot locate any upsetting feelings at all, no matter how hard they try, those emotions associated with their original story can never ever be triggered again because the moment in which that upsetting feeling first occurred can never be exactly duplicated. The individual can never again be the same as the individual was at the moment the upsetting event occurred. And the individual's perception of, and reaction to the event, and everything connected with that event changes as well.

In addition, there are bonuses in store for them. When the number is zero, their imagination simultaneously destroys anything else symbolically or metaphorically associated with that particular pattern they just destroyed. They will become aware of many other positive experiences unfolding in other parts of their lives over time, seemingly unrelated to the work you did together. It is great to finally have 'side effects' that are positive!

However, at some point in the process, many people's assessment of their associated upsetting emotions will not change; the number will not drop. If the number remains the same, say they report a four, and you light up their central pathway and they report a four again, you will then move to the next step of directing them to call upon their imagination. In this case, you may want to ask them if they are more aware of an uncomfortable feeling in their body, such as their chest, stomach, throat, arm, etc. than an upsetting emotion at this moment. If so, instruct them to tell their imagination, and not themselves, to give them an image that makes them feel that discomfort. If they have no uncomfortable feelings in their body, continue addressing the intensity of the upsetting emotions they began with. The one exception is at the very beginning when they report the original number, say at a nine, and you light up their central pathway, and they still report it at a nine. Light up their central pathway one more time and it will usually start to drop. They are simply adjusting to a process they have never experienced before.

Use the imagination method described in the following paragraphs to destroy these patterns. You will soon become aware that you will often alternate between calling upon their imaginations and lighting up their central pathways. Your work is completed when their emotional intensity goes to zero, and they cannot connect with the original, upsetting attached emotions. If they continue to rank it as a one or two over and over, have them use any one of the three "quiet your mind" statements above while they are looking at the original upsetting memory. This will help to quiet their mind and the numbers will drop.

Let these sessions reap deep payoffs as they are destroying pattern after pattern that has run them and tried to convince them there was no hope to break these lifetime patterns. Do not let a pattern's fighting for its existence get to you. Remember, remain detached from the outcome. Keep your cool. Relax. The patterns are trying to convince you and those you are working with that the patterns cannot be destroyed. Remind the people you are helping that they rule in their imagination and can destroy each and every one of those parasitical conniving patterns. Let us move onto implementing the power of the imagination.

Step 4. Using the Imagination:

In many cases, lighting up people's central pathways by itself will not reduce their assessment of the associated emotions to zero. In that case, have them ask their imaginations to conjure up an image, figure, character, object, person, monster, cartoon, etc. that is *making them* feel the emotional pain associated with their story. It is critical that they *do not think up* an answer, as there is nothing at all for them to do but to wait for their imaginations to spontaneously present them an image in response to their request. The imagination's intention is to bring about complete benefit and balance.

Explain to the people you are working with that they will receive an answer from their imagination just like they would if they used an on-line search engine or asked someone for directions to a destination. Upon asking for directions they have nothing to do. They would remain quiet until they receive an answer. The same is true when asking the imagination to produce an image for them. They should sit there quietly like a five-year-old waiting to be surprised by an image that comes to their mind spontaneously, without their ever needing to think.

Once they have received an image, have them ask the image quietly in their mind so you don't hear it: "What is your purpose (image) to make me feel, say nervous, intimidated, frustrated with myself?" If it is a positive response, you would have them tell that image to transform itself into the most positive image with the most positive energy that can reconnect them back to the "all better " feelings they told you they want to have. If they feel positive looking at that image or it communicates by itself in a positive manner, have them welcome that image to come inside their heart, spirit and every cell in their body.

However, if their imaginations respond in one of the ten ways you will read about later that represent the ten universal patterns' responses indicating it has no intention of helping them, tell them to destroy that image. They could burn or shred it like a photo, smash to smithereens as if it were made of fragile glass, dissolve it in acid, or pop it like a balloon, etc. Do not take their word that the image is destroyed. Ask them to describe how they destroyed the image and what the result was. It is critical that they see the remains of the destroyed image in front of them. Destruction in the form of burying the image, putting it into a garbage disposal, sending it off into space, etc. without seeing it actually destroyed in front of them, are tricks of the pattern to remain in control.

After successfully destroying the negative image, have them ask their imagination, and not themselves, to give them the most positive image with the most positive energy that reconnects them back to the all better feelings they desire, such as joy, inner peace, calmness, relief, happiness, exhilaration, etc. If they feel positive looking at that image or it communicates by itself in a positive manner, have them welcome that image to come inside their heart, spirit and every cell in their body.

The following sections contain the detailed, step-by-step 'how-to' instructions for destroying repeating patterns, invisible opponents, using the power of the imagination.

Imagine All Better offers you freedom.

19

The Power of Imagination

> *"Symbols have the capacity to touch us not on an intellectual level, but on behavioral and emotional levels as well."*
>
> — ALBERT EINSTEIN

BEGIN BY TELLING the people you are working with that you are going to walk them through a process in their imagination where they have total control as the director, producer, leading lady or leading man, camera person, etc. Let them know they have nothing to do as their imaginations will do everything for them. They will simply be an *observer* of images presented to them by their imaginations and only need to report to you what they observe. It's that easy. You will offer them questions, directions and suggestions to repeat to their imaginations, and their imaginations will spontaneously respond with images. They are never to enter this process with presupposed images, such as, "Oh. I know what the answer is."

The process is about allowing their imaginations, and not their rational intellects, to respond.

Imagination does not deal in logic. It has no restrictions or rules. There are no rights or wrongs. It is impossible to make a mistake working in the imagination as its *advanced intelligence* presents symbolic images that represent whatever questions, enquiries and directives are requested of it. The images that their imaginations present to them symbolize something that is not to be understood or analyzed, even though some people you are working with, or you, would love to do so. Analysis is a trap set by patterns. Your analytical left brain believes its intelligence is superior, and that it can understand what the symbolic images mean. However, symbolic images are neither this nor that, neither specific nor abstract, but something that lies in between.

While a picture speaks a thousand words, a symbolic image communicates an entire holographic history of any emotional, mental, medical, physical or spiritual problem, including, but not limited to all the feelings, words, tonalities, smells, textures and tastes all wrapped up neatly into one image. Your imagination can capture the moment a pattern originally entered you by asking your imagination for an image to appear that represents that unique point in time, regardless if you remember it or not. And even if you do recollect it, do not return to your personal history for an answer, but let your imagination, and not you, do all the work. That is the imagination's job, and not yours.

Accessing the Imagination's Wisdom for Achieving Balance

Now that the person you are working with has established a particular situation, event, person, group of people or even themselves that triggers associated feelings of angst, fear, sadness, frustration, overwhelmed, unhappiness, etc., ask them what feelings they would rather have if that situation were 'all better'. Remember, do not accept descriptions of all better feelings such as 'better', 'okay', 'stress-free', 'great', 'fine', etc. Have them be more specific in terms of how they would feel, i.e. happy, peaceful, ecstatic, safe, relaxed, relieved, free, open, confident, etc.

Get ready to enter the landscape of their imagination. You will be as fascinated as they will be as this inner journey unfolds. It is fun to do, and you will be in awe of the superior intelligence of the imagination and its delightful sense of humor; the imagination is very playful. Remind the people you work with that it is their imaginations, and not themselves, that will manifest the responses. Suggest they forget about their problem for the moment, shut down their thinking factories, just go blank, and allow their imaginations to do what the imagination does best. Have them report the very first image their imaginations presents them while they remain as passive observers with nothing at all to do. Within seconds, most of them will report an image that spontaneously comes to mind. Or they may ask you to repeat the entire question, which is perfectly fine to do. It may take repeating these instructions a second time until they are ready to go forward. Many times they will have received an image, but discount it. If they say nothing happened, remind them that their mind is always processing information and to tell you where their mind drifted off to. They may then report they had an image but "thought" it wasn't the *correct* one. Have them tell you what it was and use it in this process. If they start to ask further questions about the process at hand or go into a narrative, direct them to stay on the path of entering their imagination and following your lead. No more discussion. Just have them do it.

Direct them to do the following quietly within their mind and not aloud: "Pretend your imagination is sitting next to you or in front of you with your eyes open or closed. Quietly in your mind, tell your imagination that you need its help. Tell your imagination for it, and not you, to give you an imagine, object, cartoon character, monster, person, situation, etc. that makes you feel those upsetting emotions you feel associated with that upsetting issue, person or situation in your life."

Ask them to report the very first image their imagination presents to them. Once they have received an image representing their problem, have them ask their imagination the following questions, quietly within their mind, while their attention remains focused on the image that appeared. There are three possible questions you can ask them that will keep them in their imagination throughout the process. Never ask any questions containing the word "why" as that will trigger their left, logical, analytical brain and take them out of the process. Be alert that some people will paraphrase these questions into why-questions or ones that have nothing to do with the question you gave them to ask their imaginations. Have them tell you what they told their imaginations to do to make sure they are not asking something you never mentioned!

For learning purposes, have them ask any one of these questions to the image and objectively report only what the image did or did not do. If the image responds in one of the ten universal patterns that you will learn about shortly, you would have them immediately destroy the image.

Asking the Imagination

There are many questions that images in the imagination will answer when you introduce the question to the people you are helping. We have found that the following three questions are the most useful ones that will produce information about a pattern's operations.

Question 1. Once the persons you are working with have received an image from their imaginations, have them ask the image *always while looking at the image,* "What is your *purpose* in making me feel, say controlled or worried?" For example, if the image they received from their imaginations were a snake associated with their speaking in public, they would ask the snake, "What is your purpose in making fearful while speaking in public?" Incorporate in this question the specific, upsetting emotions they have already told you.

Question 2. While they are focused on the image, have them ask it, "How does it *benefit* you personally, for example, to make me crave food or something else that I know is not in my best interest?" Another example of anxiety associated with a boss would be to ask the image of their boss, "How does it benefit you to make me feel intimidated asking for a raise?"

Question 3. While they are looking at an image, have them ask it, "What is your *intention*, for example, in making me have relationships that never work out or making me think negatively all the time?" Or, you can rephrase it in a positive manner, "Is it your intention to make me feel relaxed and happy?" The image will usually give a straightforward Yes or No in some manner. For example, "Is it your intention for me to be happy again?" will produce a Yes or No response from the image either verbally, visually, or they will intuitively sense it is here to help them or not. If the image is negative, it will respond, "No" in some manner, i.e. it remains silent, does nothing, stays the same, talks on and on, ignores them by looking away or even disappears, shrugs, becomes mean, tries to attack them, etc. If so, tell them to destroy the image. If the image is a person or an animal, remind them that the images are symbolic, and let them know they are not harming a real person or animal by doing so.

You are directing people like actors through this process, and they rely on your being firm in doing so. You need to be firm because the pattern you are addressing in the form of an image does not want to be exposed and will do everything in its power to stay in total control. The persons you are working with are to report *only* what the image does or does not do, and never their interpretations or assumptions of what the image means, especially if the image is somebody they know. If the image is a person, such as their mother or father, they may create a story of what they believe the image is 'thinking' or 'feeling'. Ask them if the image, itself, actually spoke those words aloud to them or not. The answer will be a Yes or a No. The image may say something, do something, do nothing, disappear, become intimidating, etc. If they say the image is angry, that may be their interpretation or analysis. Have them tell you specifically what the image, itself, actually did or did not do to make them say it was angry, without adding their interpretations.

The Imagination's Answers

After having him ask his imagination for an image, a red flag for you to pay attention to is if he uses the word 'think' as in, "I think the image is ...". "Think" implies he may be in his left brain trying to understand and make sense of the image. If need be, repeat the question and suggest he do nothing while waiting for the image to respond. He has nothing to do; his imagination will do it all. For example, he may report that the image is staring straight ahead, laughing, has smoke coming out its ears, speaking words that he doesn't understand, turning away from him, spinning around, holding him in a vise, attacking him, says "No", etc. Or the image may smile warmly, wink, give him a thumbs-up signal, get brighter, say "Yes", etc.

If he remains quiet for more than 15 seconds after asking the image a question, he may have inadvertently entered a conversation with the image or initiated a separate process. Interrupt him and ask what the image did. Sometimes you will have to say, "Hello. Can you hear me? Is there anybody in there?" That may take him out of wherever he went in his mind. He is only to ask the image the questions you initiate. Do not get seduced by a pattern in you, either, such as becoming a people-pleaser that would allow him to do anything other than what you asked him to do. The pattern would love to have both of you start to analyze the image and get off course. You are in charge. Be firm. Do not let him or the pattern running him take you off course. The last thing a pattern wants is to be uncovered and destroyed.

If the image responds to any of the questions with a "Maybe", "Perhaps", or words to that effect, it is a crazy-maker. Remember as a child when you asked a parent or caretaker if he or she would take you to the beach, mountains, circus or amusement park the coming weekend, and you got a "maybe" for an answer? "Maybe" implied it may never happen. "Maybe" leaves the door open for the image to come back later and convince you that you will never get rid of the pattern. The image is either for or against you; there are no grey areas of "maybe" or "perhaps". If this is the image's response, annihilate the image. You are destroying the parasitic pattern housed in the image that has no intention of helping.

An exception would be if his imagination produced an image of himself at his current age, or even younger, as the culprit who is responsible for creating all of his problems. It is never the image of the person himself with whom you are working who is at fault, ever. The pattern's playing games have tricked him into believing that he is the one sabotaging his life. The patterns are trying to throw him under the wheels of a bus by presenting him as the guilty party. Never have him destroy images of himself. Here is the way to deal with an image of himself.

As he looks at the image of himself, have him tell that image to transform itself into the most positive image with the most positive energy that reconnects him to feeling the positive emotions he wishes to have, i.e. happy, relieved, safe, etc. If he receives a favorable response, then have him welcome that new positive image to come into his heart, his spirit and every cell in his body.

There will be times when the person you are helping will receive an image from his imagination that makes him unable to tell if the image is here to help him or not. This situation may occur after he has destroyed an image and then tells his imagination to give him the most positive image with the most positive energy that reconnects him back to feeling the positive emotions he selected, such as happy, relaxed and confident.

Ask the person if he intuitively feels good or not good looking at that image and you will usually receive a "Yes" or a "No". If he is not a hundred percent certain that image is here to help him or not, have him tell that image: "I am not 100% sure if you are here to help me or not. So transform into another image that will let me know one way or the other if you are here to help me or not." That new image will be easy to test because it will intuitively feel good or not good. If it feels good, it means that the original image in question was here to help that person all along. Then you would have him invite that original image to come inside his heart, spirit and every cell in his body.

However, if he feels that the new image is negative or not good, that lets you know the original image in question is not good, either. So, have him destroy that original image, and have his imagination give him the most positive image with the most positive energy that can reconnect him to the positive emotions he previously selected. And if that image feels good, have him welcome it to come inside his heart, spirit and every cell in his body.

Misguided Images and Educating Images

The use of these three questions will elicit spontaneous symbolic images from their imaginations giving various responses. However, not all images represent a pattern. Sometimes the images are *'misguided'* believing they were helping or protecting you all along, while other images may need to be *'educated'* as to the price you have been paying emotionally, physically, mentally and spiritually with that image in your imagination. However, if the image's response to any of these three questions comes under the heading of any of the ten universal patterns you will learn about in the next chapter, annihilate the image. Annihilation techniques will be discussed later as well. You are never destroying a living entity, even if the adversary's image appears in the form of a person or animal. Those images are symbolic and represent a psychic virus or invisible opponent.

Let's address the images that are misguided and those images that need to be educated. Misguided images' intentions are well-meaning. They believe what they are doing is beneficial for you in terms of making you feel safe and protected or successful and happy. For example, if you have fear of driving, a misguided image will respond to questions you ask them that their purpose in keeping you anxious and fearful is to protect you from driving and being hurt or killed. They usually do not go into such detail, but may say their purpose is to "Protect" or make you feel "Safe". In this case, look at the image and tell it in your own mind, and not aloud, that you are in agreement with its overall intention of keeping you protected, but not how it is going about doing it by generating fear and anxiety to protect you.

Then educate the image as if you were a teacher educating a five-year-old for the first time. Tell the image that you are feeling anything but protected when thinking about driving or when you are behind the wheel. Educate the image while looking at it how you are feeling emotionally. As you are looking at the image in your mind, quietly say to yourself and not aloud, for example, "I feel nervous; I feel scared; I feel butterflies in my stomach; I feel clammy hands; I feel chest pains; I feel upset; etc." Do not go into a narrative or blame the image.

When you educate an image, it will *always* do one of two things. It will either <u>verbally</u> respond in a way that acknowledges you by being sympathetic, understanding or compassionate. Sometimes it even becomes sad or tearful. Or, it will do nothing, stare at you, remain the same, ignore you be turning away or disappearing, get mad, believe it is right and you are wrong, be stern or talk on and on and on. If it is any of these negative responses, destroy the image.

Let's use fear of flying as another example that shows how an invisible opponent, a repeating pattern, has taken over and it, and not you, is generating your fear. While questioning the image regarding its intention or purpose, ask it, "Are you here to help me to feel safe *and* feel relaxed about flying?" If it responds positively, tell the image that you will show it how it can help you. Now, since you are the director in your imagination, you will give the image a directive, that is, you will direct it so it can help you. Tell the image, "In order to help me feel protected while flying, transform yourself into the most positive image with the most positive energy that makes me feel safe and relaxed when flying." And if a positive image appears in your mind, welcome it to come inside you. If it is a negative one, destroy it and tell your imagination for it, and not you, to give you the most positive image with the most positive energy to make you feel safe and relaxed. And then welcome that positive image to come inside you.

Educating an image from the very beginning is helpful if the image is a person you know. For example, whenever you receive an image of a person you know, say a coach, boss, friend, parent, sibling, etc., you will want to educate their image. While you are looking at the image of that person quietly in your mind, only tell the image how you feel. Do not go into a narrative or blame the image. Don't tell the image of that person that he or she *makes* you feel your upsetting feelings. Only educate the image while looking at it: "I feel..." followed by one feeling after another feeling. For example, "I feel annoyed; I feel anxious; I feel demeaned; I feel not good enough; I feel sad; I feel invalidated, etc." Opening up to these people and being candid with how you feel - and not that *they* are responsible for making you feel your emotions – may be the first time you have done so from an "I" point of view.

Be highly aware whenever an image does nothing, stays the same or stares at you, where you find yourself making up a story that the image "heard me" or was "sympathetic or understanding of me", when in fact the image actually did or said nothing. If so, imagine that image as if it were a photograph or picture and burn it with a match or shred it, or destroy it any way you want. Then tell your imagination to give you the most positive image with the most positive energy to reconnect you back to feeling the positive emotions you chose.

If any of the persons' images you are educating about how you feel respond with a *verbal* communication that they are sympathetic, compassionate and understanding of your situation, nods their head in a yes manner, smiles warmly, etc., then thank the image and tell it that you will show it how to help you feel better. As you look at the image of that person, tell it to transform itself into the most positive image with the most positive energy that makes you feel whatever those all-better feelings would be, i.e. acknowledged, happy, relaxed, etc. If the image transforms into a positive image, then thank it and welcome it to come inside you. However, if its intention is negative, then annihilate the image. Again, the most benign way to annihilate the symbolic image of a person you know is by pretending the image is a piece of film or a photo and shred it or put a match to it. Or if you chose, pretend the person's image is made of fragile glass and smash it to smithereens. Remember, images of people are only symbolic and you are in no way harming the actual person. You are simply communicating to your imagination that you don't want what that person's image symbolically represents. You can then ask your imagination to replace it with a positive image.

The Dating Game All Better

Virginia lived in Atlanta and had just turned 30. Her perplexing situation had to do with breaking up with two men she had been dating for only short periods of time. She said, "I have a pattern that makes me find myself guarded around men. I put up a wall and recede while I check them out to see if they're OK. I become very cold and detached in doing so. I'm also afraid to express myself, my feelings. I feel incompetent to act as my normal, decent self. I become intense, anxious and standoffish. I even avoid eye contact." Virginia's goal was to feel, "Relaxed. Present. In my body. Light-hearted and having fun around men."

On a zero-to-10 scale, Virginia's anxious and intense feelings were reported as 10. As I lit her central pathway, she reported her numbers dropping to a five, a two and a one. It did not move below one. So I had her call upon her imagination, which presented her an image of a book keeping her fearful and disconnected when dating. The book said that its purpose in making her so guarded and anxious when it came time to dating men was to keep her "safe". Virginia was in agreement with the book's intention to feel safe as well. I told her that sometimes the images are misguided and believe they mean well by being over protective.

I told her, "As you look at the book in your mind's eye, let the book know that you are in total agreement with its bottom line of wanting you to feel safe as you want to feel safe as well. I want you to educate the book without blaming it. Tell the book that its intention for you to feel safe is not working. While looking at the book, educate it exactly what you are feeling emotionally and physically, which is anything but safe when you are dating men. Tell the book how *you* feel and not that the book makes you feel this. Do not blame the book. Educate the book's image about being afraid to express yourself, your anxiety and fear to look a young man in his eyes, and what goes on inside your body, such as tension, butterflies in your stomach, etc. And what a living nightmare it is for you whenever you venture into the dating game. I'll be quiet while you educate the book how you feel and let me know when you finish doing so."

Whenever you educate a symbolic image, such as an object or person, it will do one of two things. It will acknowledge you, smile warmly, verbally communicate compassionately and sympathetically, or sometimes becomes sad or even teary-eyed. Or the image will ignore you, blame you, become angry or talk on and on and on. It is always good to remind the positive responding image that you are not blaming it since its intention was well-meaning all along. Virginia reported, "It's sympathetic to me." I had her ask the book if its intention was to keep her safe, relaxed and connected whenever dating, and she received a "Definitely" from the book.

I asked her to thank the book and tell the book that you are going to show it how to help you. As she looked at the book's image, I asked her to say, "Book. Transform yourself into the most positive image with the most positive energy that can reconnect me to my original spirit of feeling relaxed, safe and enjoy the experience of meeting and dating men." She said, "It became a big, brown horse" and added, "I feel powerful, and light, and feminine." Virginia welcomed the image of the horse to come inside her heart, her spirit and every cell in her body. She could not find any skeptic to make her doubt the positive intention of the horse.

I had her return to the original upsetting memory in her mind and rank it again on a zero-to-10 scale and evaluate what number those intense feelings of being guarded, anxious and fearful to express her feelings around men she was dating. She said it was a two. However, a memory with some pain associated with it came to mind immediately. I had her imagination transform that specific painful memory into an image and it gave her a piece of chocolate. (All you chocolate lovers, like me, don't freak out.) The symbol of chocolate in Virginia's imagination was associated with pain on some symbolic level. The image of chocolate said it had no intention of helping her, so Virginia was told to destroy it. Upon doing so, her imagination came up with a positive image of making her feel comfortable dating, and she said, "It's a tropical fish. I feel good looking at it as there is good light, and the image can move freely." The intensity of her discomfort on the zero-to-10 scale dropped and stayed at a zero. She could not make herself feel any of the original upsetting emotions.

Virginia left the following message a week later on my phone: "I'm feeling great. I feel fantastic. I've had some breakthroughs in the areas we discussed. I am very pleased. I feel very light and carefree. I appreciate your help." When we spoke in person she mentioned, "I feel separate from the emotions associated with all the drama that was going on. Even with men, my guard is let down. Now I'm safe. It's weird how I feel different. The drama is gone. In the past I didn't strike up conversations with men. But the other day I had eye contact and was able to talk to a guy. We were both flirting. It feels so normal." Virginia offered several metaphors describing the Imagine All Better approach: "It's like a frontal lobotomy with your emotions. It just snipped the emotions. It clipped my brain in half. It clipped that connection working overtime in a nasty way. It was all about breaking patterns."

The following diagram shows the sequence of steps to follow in order to destroy a pattern:

IMAGINE ALL BETTER

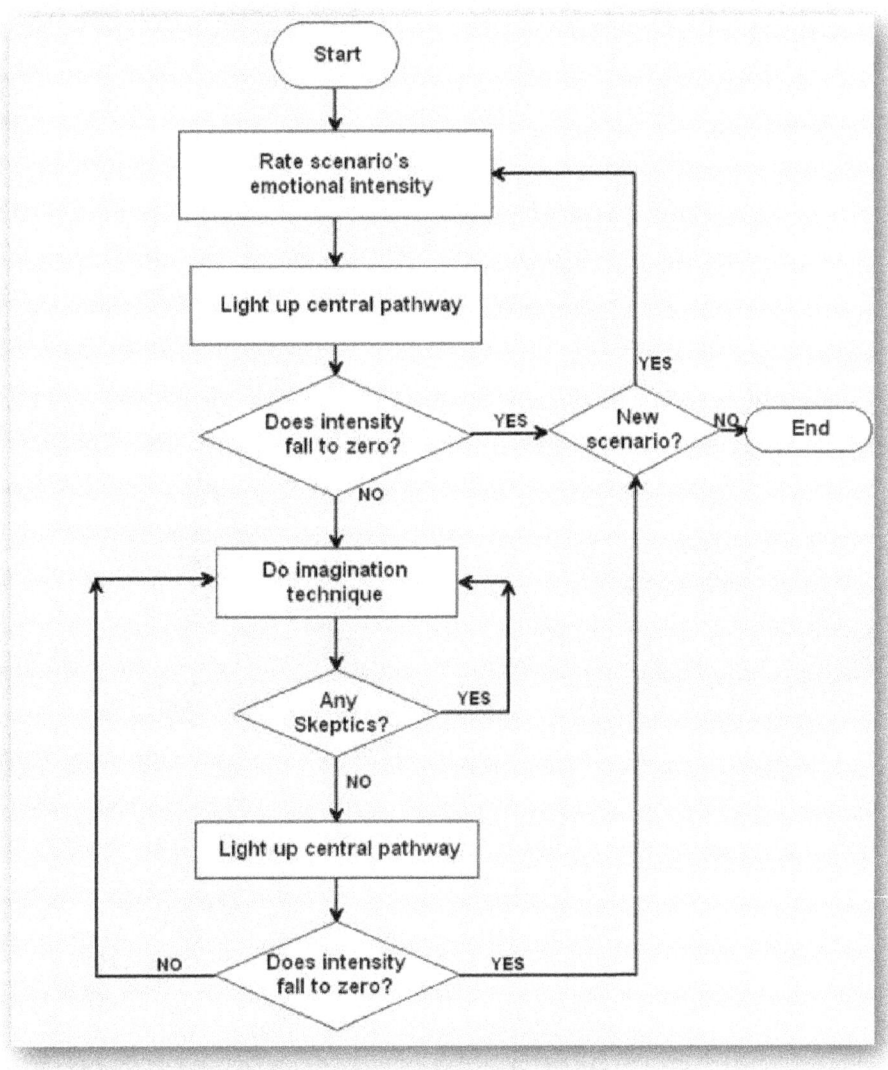

The following chapters contain the detailed, step by step 'how-to' instructions for destroying patterns using the imagination.

Imagine All Better offers you freedom.

20

Wanted Dead or Dead-Dead: Ten Universal Patterns Found in Your Unconscious

"Whatever you bury, you bury alive."

— Anonymous

THE NIAGARA FALLS' Love Canal environmental disaster that took place years ago is an analogy of the expression, "Whatever you bury; you bury alive." Unbeknownst to its 1300 residents, their houses were built upon a chemical dump yard. It took two decades before 22,000 tons of buried chemical wastes surfaced. Its toxicity resulted in a high incidence of cancer from chromosomal damage to many of the Love Canal residents.

There are ten invisible opponents that present themselves in the form of repeating upsetting emotional and behavioral patterns that you will learn how to uncover and destroy. The images that manifest from the imagination are different from person to person. When a person asks specific questions of the imagination, the imagination complies immediately with images in a manner similar to the fable of the magical genie in the bottle: "Your wish is my command."

Ten Universal Patterns

It is amazing how connected we all are. The following classic patterns' responses are found worldwide in everybody's imaginations:

1) Nothing Response
2) Accusatory
3) Misery Loves Company
4) Fun
5) It's My Job
6) Power and Control
7) Kill and Destroy
8) Indifference
9) Parasite
10) Attitude

NOTHING RESPONSE

The Nothing Response pattern responds by doing nothing, stays the same, stares at you, shakes its head No, etc. If the image does not communicate directly with you, don't *think* it is listening to you or understands what you are going through. That's a story you are making up in your mind. By not receiving any response from the image, it may make you start to think: "Maybe I'm doing this process incorrectly" or "I don't understand the question." The pattern's response of 'nothing' matches what the pattern does in your current life's situation. A Nothing Response from the image promotes doubt. Your mind begins to over think and you get overwhelmed with analysis. Destroy it.

ACCUSATORY
The Accusatory pattern throws the problem back onto you. Instead of answering the question asked, the image blames you by saying something to the effect, "*You're* doing it to *yourself*," or "Because *you* don't believe in *yourself*", or "It's *you* making *yourself* have the problem". While there will be variations on the images' responses, the response always includes the words "you", "your", "you're" or "yourself" at the beginning, middle or end of its response to you. The image gives you the feeling of a finger pointing at you and accusing you as the one responsible for your problem. Do not become conned by the pattern when it communicates back to you in such an accusatory manner. Destroy it.

MISERY LOVES COMPANY
The Misery Loves Company pattern implies that its life is not doing well either. It is miserable. It is not having any enjoyment in its life; its life sucks too. Or it is all alone and has nobody in the world except you. It wants you to feel sorry for it and join its misery, as misery loves company. Destroy it.

FUN
The Fun pattern responds with expressions such as, "Fun", "Funny", "It's fun", or "I have fun doing this to you," etc. It derives its "fun" and pleasure at your expense. It is like you are its TV sitcom when it is bored and wants to stir up your emotions, just for the fun of it. It likes to tease and taunt you and have fun at your expense. Destroy it.

IT'S MY JOB
The It's My Job pattern will respond in one of the following ways: "It's who I am." "It's what I do." "It's my job." "It's my nature." "I do it because I can.", or "Because I just do it." For example, if it were an image of a vise, and you asked its intention, it may respond: "It's what I do," implying, "What part of this don't you get? I'm a vise for crying out loud.

Think for a moment what the heck a vise's purpose is? It's who I am and what I do. Now do you get it? It's my job." Destroy it.

POWER & CONTROL
The Power and Control pattern responds in one of two ways: "power" or "control" or similar words. This pattern's intention is to control you and have dominion and power over you. Destroy it.

KILL & DESTROY
The Kill and Destroy pattern is clear. It says it is here to "kill" or "destroy" you. Do not take its response personally. It is only an image in your imagination where you rule completely. For example, if an image wanting to kill you had a weapon, you can take the weapon away and use it destroy the image. A classic image is the devil holding a pitchfork. Destroy it.

INDIFFERENCE
The Indifference pattern disavows you. When asked a question, the image ignores you. It may turn away from you; it may disappear or walk away from you, or it may continue doing what it is doing as if it never heard you ask a question. The Indifference pattern also presents itself with an image shrugging its shoulders, turning its palms over or putting its hands up in the air. Destroy it.

PARASITE
The Parasite pattern responds: "I exist at your expense." "It makes me exist." "It makes me happy" by making you unhappy. It gets stronger by keeping you weaker. It leeches your life force. Destroy it.

ATTITUDE
The Attitude pattern has a chip on its shoulder. It has major attitude. It is cocky; It may have a smirky smile or a mean, smart-aleck grin; it may swear or spit at you; it puts its hands on its hips or crosses its arms; it may growl

at you: it may attack you; it may laugh and cackle at you; it may intimidate you, etc. Destroy it.

A Lifetime of Being Bullied All Better

A pattern of being bullied can last a lifetime. Crystal is a vivacious 39-year-old, happy-go-lucky, bright, humorous woman who works in the film industry. She called because she had issues with Tiffany, her new business partner and co-producer of her next film. Tiffany had befriended Crystal, who had charisma and contacts with all the major studios, along with an impressive track record of successful films. The sweet and endearing Tiffany had a hidden agenda all along, and a hidden personality that emerged once they had a legal contract between them of being partners as co-producers. Crystal found Tiffany becoming controlling, manipulative and mean at times. She had a gnawing feeling that Tiffany was mismanaging money from investors, and possibly having two sets of books. Whenever Crystal commented upon it, Tiffany would throw a hissy fit and make her feel like she was crazy with such insinuations. Crystal would always back down.

Crystal only had a short period of time to work with me over the phone because she was packing to go back east where the film was being shot. She mentioned several words that came to mind to describe her feelings about Tiffany: afraid, apprehensive and mad. Since she was in such a rush, I asked her which one she wanted to work on. She selected her being mad.

"On a scale of zero-to-10 just how intense is your anger? The higher the numbers go, the angrier and more upset you are at her."

"Why limit me to ten?", she said laughing.

"Ten means if you were a serial killer, she would be your cereal this morning for breakfast."

"It's a humongous number ten."

"OK. Now hold onto that memory where your anger is that high."

While Crystal did that, I remotely lit up her central pathway with gold light, and she reported her numbers dropping to a 5 immediately, then a 2 and a zero.

"It felt like air coming out of a balloon as the numbers dropped."

"Is there any feeling, no matter how small, still left there with any anger or being mad?"

"Just a tiny bit is left. It's in my stomach."

"Tell your imagination for it, and not you Crystal, to come up with an image, a symbol, a cartoon character, a person, a monster... something or somebody that is giving you that feeling in your stomach."

"It's a black creature with arms and legs sticking out of it."

"Ask it, 'What is your purpose making my stomach upset?'"

"It walked away from me."

"That response is one of the ten patterns I call 'indifference'. In your imagination, you rule; you run the show. It's like our parents used to say: 'It's my house and you have to go by my rules.' Well, everything and everyone in the house of your imagination has to go by your rules. Tell that character that walked away from you to get its ass back pronto. Be firm and annoyed with her image as you tell it what to do. Remember that you are the producer, director, and leading lady in your imagination."

"When I raised my voice and screamed at it, it shrunk very small."

"Ask that image if its intention is to help calm down your stomach?"

"It said No."

"Kill it. Destroy it. Anything that is not here to support you unconditionally in your imagination is a pattern."

"I jumped up and down on it, but it won't die."

"Ask your imagination's help to come up with a way that will destroy it once and for all."

"Done! I dynamited it to pieces, and then I poured acid on. It's definitely destroyed now."

"That symbolic image just experienced what I call a psychic death. How would you like your stomach to feel?"

"Safe. Peaceful."

"Tell your imagination to conjure up the most positive image with the most positive energy that reconnects you back to your original spirit of feeling totally safe and peaceful."

"It's the Statue of Liberty."

"How does your stomach feel while looking at the Statue of Liberty?"

"Relaxed. I feel protected. Sure of myself. The Statue of Liberty becomes more like a winged character now."

"Welcome the winged Statue of Liberty to come inside your heart, your spirit and every cell in your body. Let me know how you feel when that happens."

"Good. I feel very light."

Go back to the original upsetting memory of being angry and mad at this woman and rank what number it is now on a zero-to-10 scale."

"I can't. I can't find it. It's like I'm in an altered state; my body feels tingling. It feels different."

"That positive altered state your feeling is called consciousness; pure awareness! You're in the moment. You were in a negative altered state with the anger that the pattern had attached to the story of you and this woman of being betrayed, cheated, etc. You'll never have that particular anger and rage which ate away at you and also made you have to eat it and hold it in all these years. From now on, whenever you think about or interact with this business woman, you will never again feel overtaken by such anger. It doesn't mean you won't feel anger again, but it won't collapse you into an old state of being a little girl who believed she had no power or choices. That's a thing of the past."

"Thanks. I'll let you know how it goes when I return from Boston."

"I look forward to hearing what else you become aware of. Welcome back to consciousness!"

Crystal's Follow-Up

When Crystal called me several days later, she was driving home from the airport, so we could not work as she needed to be focused. I suggested she reviewed her history with other females with whom she experienced similar oppositional energy like her current business partner who were jealous, betrayed her or manipulated her.

She left me a voice message the next evening wanting a second session to deal with "the evil one." Even though she felt a huge shift from our initial work, she knew there was something still operating as she felt some apprehension and fear – the emotions we didn't have time to address during our initial session. The pattern of anger was dismantled. Now it's time to do the same thing with the pattern of apprehension and fear running her.

"I've paid close attention to what you suggested regarding negative, female energy in my life. I know where that pattern began. There was this scary girl I knew from grades two through six. I was always nice to her. But suddenly, in the sixth grade she turned against me for no reason. She would chase me, make fun of me and even beat me up numerous times. My parents would see me coming home from school crying, and I never told them what was happening. Isn't that weird? I held it all inside. Years later, I learned that this mean girl's father used to physically beat her."

"How would you like to feel instead"?

"Centered. Grounded."

I had an intuitive sense that her current issue dealt with someone from her childhood. However, most times the person I'm working with has no idea on earth where it came from. I've known Crystal for many years and remember different events in her life with issues of female friends who somehow turned against her. Her quandary was always that she had no idea what she ever did or said to make these friends behave negatively toward her. Tiffany was but one more example of a female who initially was a friend and then turned into one who bullied her and controlled her with intimidation.

What I usually do is ask a person to have their imagination come up with an image that represents the very first time in their life when they originally felt those intense upsetting emotions. In Crystal's situation, it was fear and apprehension. That question sets the imagination to go into motion to recreate the original 'point of entry' of a repeating pattern visa vie a symbolic image. The image contains the history in all its detail without words or analysis. That's the beauty of this approach.

IMAGINE ALL BETTER

"Crystal, let's get started. What is the number on a zero-to-10 scale where zero is being completely centered and grounded, and the higher the number goes the more you find yourself feeling apprehensive and fearful with the particular memory of that bully."

"It's a 10."

As I lit up her central pathway, Crystal reported the numbers dropping until they got to a five and wouldn't drop lower. Since her issue dealt with a particular person, I simply asked her to imagine the young girl in question.

"As you look at the image of that 6th grade girl in your imagination, ask her, 'How does it benefit you to make me feel so apprehensive and fearful?'"

"She's just smiling at me."

"Like a sarcastic, smirky, arrogant smile?"

"Exactly. How did you know that?"

"I've done this over 100,000 times. That smirky look on her face is what I call an 'attitude' character, which is one of ten worldwide patterns. These responses of symbolic images are classic, universal responses that come from everyone's collective unconscious. As you look at the girl again, ask her, 'What is your intention in wanting to scare me?'"

"To hurt you."

"Dismantle her; destroy her; zap her. Remember you are not killing or destroying a living human being, but rather an organic, parasitical pattern that's been running your fear and causing you these repetitive problems during your life, including the issue at hand with your business partner."

"Okay. I pretended she was a photograph and I burned her. Everything burned except her left hand remains there. I don't know what to do."

"That's the pattern wanting you to believe that you have no power to overcome it. Pretend her left hand is made of glass like a fragile figurine and smash it."

"Done. It's smashed to pieces."

"Now tell you imagination for it, and not you, to welcome back the most positive image with the most positive energy that can reconnect you to your original spirit of feeling centered and grounded."

"A big white horse with wings, like a Pegasus. It's beautiful; it's overwhelming. Like it's my higher Self that's grounded. And it now lifts me out of my old upsetting feeling. And it just entered me on its own. It must have read your mind about your next suggestion you'd be asking me to do! I'm now on its back and we're going on a ride, like everything's okay. A whole other life."

"Go back to the original upsetting memory of that 6th grade bully and on a zero-to-ten scale, what number is the intensity of those upsetting feelings now."

"It's a five and all of a sudden I'm feeling a pain in my stomach, like a knot in my stomach."

"Ask your imagination to come up with an image that is giving you that feeling in your stomach."

"It's that same girl with a knife."

"Whenever the image is threatening, like she is, you can make yourself invisible and reappear in a safe place in your imagination looking at her."

"OK."

"Good. Now ask her, 'What is your intention in giving me the pain in my stomach?'"

"I want you dead."

"That's an example of the accusatory pattern as it will use 'you', 'your', or 'you're' at the beginning, middle or end of its reply."

"Don't take what she said seriously as you are in your imagination where you're in charge and not the image. Consider taking the knife from her and then somehow destroy her with her own weapon. I think that's a fitting ending to this symbolic pattern."

"On my God. I sawed her head off with the knife!"

"I can see this scene in the next film you produce. Now ask your imagination, and not yourself, to come up with the most positive image with the most positive energy that can reconnect you back to your original spirit of feeling grounded and centered."

"It's a bearded man. Like Jesus."

"Asked that image, 'Are you here to help me reconnect to feeling centered and grounded again?'"

"He smiles warmly and nods his head."

"Then welcome the image of Jesus to come inside your heart, your spirit and every cell in your body to be with you now and forever so you can be at peace and centered."

"Done."

"Back to the zero-to-10 scale Crystal. What number is that pain in your stomach now?"

"It's a three."

I only had to light up her central pathway a couple of times before she reported it as a zero.

"Now go back to that same memory of that intimidating 6th grade girl and see what upsetting emotions or uncomfortable physical sensations you are aware of having."

"Can't find it. It's not there anymore. Oh, there's the conference call coming in, I gotta go now. That was perfect timing."

Next time I spoke with Crystal, she was laughing and said, "After I was into the second call with 'the evil one', I almost started laughing when a big smile came over me. I don't know why. The conversation was becoming so ridiculous. Tiffany started freaking out, and it didn't make me flinch at all. I felt so detached from the way I used to feel with her that the conversation seemed funnier and funnier as it went on.

I have an entertainment attorney reviewing our contract that she had her attorney write in the first place, and I never questioned it. I've never done that before. I always had it reviewed by my attorney. It was like she had a spell over me for trusting her blindly. During the phone call, I was a different person: clear and present without any butterflies, anger or fear. I'm good now."

Imagine All Better offers you freedom.

21

Annihilation Technique

*"Canst thou not minister to a mind diseased,
Pluck from the memory a rooted sorrow,
Raze out the written troubles of the brain,
And with some sweet oblivious antidote
Cleanse the stuffed blossom of that perilous stuff
Which weights upon the heart?"*

— SHAKESPEARE

WE ARE ALL familiar with the fable *Hansel and Gretel* and the classic *Wizard of Oz* where the heroes needed to annihilate the witches to have their freedom. The death or annihilation of an adversary in the imagination, followed by the rebirth of an ally is a necessary step. It causes the adversary's energy to emerge as a skillful servant to a person. Destroying an internal foe is not equivalent to murder of a person or animal in the external world. The annihilation of an adversary, which merely symbolizes a harmful pattern, is like the annihilation of harmful bacteria by an antibiotic. The death of a malicious pattern releases beneficial energy from the part of the person you are working with that had formed into the adversary's symbolic image. Energy does not die; it can only change form. A symbolic death of an internal adversary allows its energy to be re-formed into an image of an inner ally.

The *Tibetan Book of Living and Dying* shows how universal birth and death is in the process of life as it is in our imagination: "Every subatomic interaction consists of the annihilation of the original particles and the creation of new subatomic particles. The subatomic world is a continual dance of creation and annihilation, of mass changing into energy and energy changing to mass."

Thich Nhat Hahn, the Vietnamese Buddhist poet and philosopher has a similar perspective on this continuous dance of life and death:

> *Earth brings us into life*
> *and nourishes us.*
> *Earth takes us back again.*
> *Birth and death are present in every moment.*

If the image's response to questions about its purpose, benefit or intention comes under the heading of any of the ten parasitical patterns, then annihilate it. While doing so, focus your attention on the image making sure it is "dead-dead", so you could sign an affidavit that it is. Sometimes the image is a trickster that will play possum and make you believe you have destroyed it, but it was only to fool you into a false sense of safety and will come back to haunt you. The pattern cunningly does this to make you believe it is impossible to ever get rid of your long-standing struggles, your personal demons. Do not be conned into such a false belief by the pattern, even when you hear *its* voice in your head telling you so, or *its* words coming out of your mouth. That internal or external voice is the voice of the pattern using you like a ventriloquist does with its dummy to spout words that appear to come from the dummy, when all along the words come from the pattern-ventriloquist itself. Imagine the pattern as a sci-fi character that is able to mimic your voice-print making you believe your thoughts and verbal expressions are coming from you. All its tricks and strategies will fail when you make the invisible pattern visible through the use of your imagination and annihilate it.

Different Ways to Kill Patterns

Your imagination is unlimited in the ways that you can use it to destroy patterns, your invisible opponents. If you are stuck, always ask your imagination for its help to annihilate a pattern. See what the people with whom you are working come up with on their own when instructed to annihilate a pattern's image. Flash back on movies, books, plays, fairy tales and mythology to help trigger ways to annihilate the pattern's image. If they get stuck, you can offer whatever comes to your mind or any of the following suggestions:

- Shred it or burn it as if it were a photo or piece of film. This is usually the suggested method if the image is a person whom they know such as a mother, father, sibling, etc.
- Shoot it.
- Pretend it is made of dry, fragile wood and break it into pieces.
- Put it through a wood chipper or a pencil sharpener.
- Pour gasoline on it and put a match to it.
- Use a flamethrower.
- Pour sulfuric acid on it.
- Zap it.
- Beat it up.
- Hit it with a bat, club, hammer, etc.
- Pretend the image is made of fragile glass like a delicate glass figurine and smash it to smithereens or imagine a boulder, cartoon-style, falls from the sky smashing it to pieces.
- Make yourself 10 times or 100 times bigger than the nasty image and crush it, destroy it, etc. You can even do this the instant an

image from your imagination makes you feel uncomfortable or intimidated.
- Sever its head with an ax or knife.
- Pretend the image is a balloon and pop it with a pin.

If an image is threatening or attacking you, make yourself disappear and reappear in your imagination in a safe place while looking at the menacing image at a safe distance and annihilate it. You can also simply disappear so the image can no longer see you and then destroy it. It literally will not know what hit it. Do not accept the image's 'reality' and how it presents itself to you ever as being impossible to destroy. It is just an image, and you can do anything to it in your imagination.

If you are feeling frustrated trying to destroy an image that does not respond, keeps returning, or has made you believe you have run out of ways to annihilate it, just ask your imagination for it to come up with another image that parallels the image at hand. Ask your imagination to give you a parallel image that is easy to destroy once and for all. You never have to accept an image that is vague, difficult to see, etc. Your imagination will give you another image that is so much easier to deal with. You are never alone in this world. You are always with an entourage of inner allies within your imagination that in a moment's notice can protect you and return balance to your life with Imagine All Better.

If an image only partially burns and some part remains, imagine that the remaining piece is fragile glass and smash it to smithereens or pour acid on it. If the image makes you believe you do not know how you can destroy it, that belief is the pattern operating in your thoughts. Imagine some figure or person who could go into battle on your behalf with the image. It may be a superhero or a magical/mystical figure such as an angel. If the negative image is that of a ghost or a cloud figure, pretend it made of glass and smash it.

If the image is vague, murky or difficult to destroy, then simply ask your imagination to give you a parallel image that represents the original image that is easy for you to destroy. Or tell your imagination to transform that image into one that you can easily destroy.

If you want to have fun with the image that still appears difficult to destroy, then ask the image, "What manner of your own death do you fear the most?" On occasion, the image will actually tell you. Other times it gets impertinent and says, "I'm not telling you. What do you think, I'm stupid or something?" Have fun with the images. Remember they are in your imagination, and you run the show there, not them.

One of your alternatives is to look directly at the image and pretend to be the psychic of all psychics in the world. Pretend you can read the image's mind as to what form of annihilation it does not want you to know, or else it would be destroyed. Then use that method to destroy the image. You can also imagine how that obstinate image would look completely destroyed.

What Not to Do When Destroying an Image

In all cases, it is critical that they see the remains of the destroyed image in front of them.

- Do not make it disappear.
- Do not put it into your mouth and eat it.
- Do not put it into a vacuum cleaner, container, rocket ship, garbage disposal, etc.
- Do not let the image disappear of its own volition or destroy itself. Annihilating it has to come from your intention of how you want to destroy it and not the image destroying itself.
- If you toss it over a cliff, make sure you see the image impaled on a sharp rock or is spattered all over the ground below. Do anything else that comes to mind.
- You always want to keep your eye on the image and see it destroyed right in front of you. If you toss the image into the ocean or a body

of water you can drain the ocean, like emptying a bathtub, and then destroy the image. Or you can do anything else that comes to mind.
- Do not chase it away or allow it to walk away on its own.
- Do not erase it.
- Oh, and do not believe this list is exhaustive. You will encounter other ways a pattern will try to trick you. Be vigilant. Let your intuition guide you. Let the Force be with you!

The Skeptic

A skeptic would be a doubt or an intuitive feeling that the image makes the person feel uncomfortable. If there is no skeptic and the person you are working feels good about the image, this particular process has ended. However, if they report a skeptic then return to the original process. You would have them ask their imagination for an image, symbol, cartoon character, object, person, place, monster, etc. that is making them feel skepticism or doubt in the manner they describe. Sometimes there may be several skeptics. Each annihilation results in peace of mind and greater freedom from patterns' operations.

After they report that a positive image has successfully entered their heart, spirit and every cell in their body, *always* ask if they are aware of a skeptic. A skeptic presents itself in different ways:

1) as a doubtful, questioning or negative voice or a "thought form" within their thoughts or
2. as a physical tension or physiological discomfort in the stomach, heart, throat, heaviness in the chest, head sensation, etc. or
3. as a feeling of fear, worry, sadness, etc. or
4. a skeptical image appears

In addition to being able to remotely light up anyone's central pathway, which is a fascinating experience, we have just added another way it can be done. You now have the choice to light up the person's central pathway in your mind's eye or tell the person you are working with to imagine lighting up her central pathway with gold light. Once the person has done so, tell her to imagine the gold light coming from her central pathway while simultaneously looking at that upsetting memory that she has already ranked on a zero-to-10 scale. After each time she does that, ask her to rank the intensity of her emotions on a zero-to-10 scale again. If the numbers continue to decrease, continue to tell her to imagine the gold light along her central pathway while looking at the upsetting memory and report what number it is. However, if she reports that the numbers no longer move lower, then have her ask her imagination to produce an image that is causing her to feel her upsetting emotions, as you would have been doing all along.

Ending Statement

Thanks for being with us. We believe you not only have a new paradigm as a change agent, but more importantly a new approach to help you, your family, friends, clients and even strangers you sit next to on airplanes. That's it for now. Keep in contact with us. Email us at info@ImagineAllBetter.com and let us know how you are doing, what questions you might have and what transformations and miracles you have been an agent for and how we can help you further. Visit us at www.ImagineAllBetter.com.

You also have the opportunity of installing our Imagine All Better app, a life-changing, "stress-relief-on-demand" mobile app that allows you, family members and friends to destroy repeating upsetting emotions and behaviors.

Imagine All Better offers you freedom.

Appendix A

Partial Listing of Patterns That Manipulate Your Life

"Between the idea and the reality, between the motion and the act, falls the Shadow."

— T.S. Eliot

SEE WHERE A pattern may currently be manipulating your life, your free will, your choices, your emotional or physical health, etc.

The following is a partial list of topics that Imagine All Better has the potential to permanently destroy.

- Addicted to social media
- Addicted to the Internet
- Afraid to take risks

- Aging parents
- All conversations are negative
- Always come in second
- Always hurting the ones I love the most
- Always late
- Always worried about my grown-up children
- Always worried about my young children
- Always worry about people's health
- Anger management
- Angry/mad at myself
- Anxiety following being robbed/mugged
- Anxiety making cold calls
- Anxiety over career
- Anxiety/depression associated with anniversary of event
- Bad habits
- Bad luck
- Battling a disease
- Becoming like my mother or father not in a good way
- Bed wetting
- Betrayed
- Biting nails
- Body-image
- Boredom
- Bridezilla
- Bullied/teased/made fun of
- Bullying others
- Can't keep New Year's resolutions
- Can't keep job/relationship for long
- Can't be alone
- Certain people get on my nerves
- Cheating on my boyfriend/girlfriend
- Children's sadness/unhappiness
- Confusion

- Control issues
- Controlled by _____
- Couples who press each other's buttons
- Cranky/crabby
- Cravings
- Cyberbulling
- Dating losers
- Demeaned by _____
- Depressed/down/blue
- Desperate
- Disappointment in myself
- Disapproved of by _____
- Divorced parents/divorce in family
- Doubt/skepticism about making choices
- Draining people
- Drama queen
- Dwelling in future
- Dwelling in past
- Dying from a terrible illness
- Easily manipulated
- Ego gets in way
- Emotional pain
- Emotionally frozen/paralyzed
- Emptiness
- Everybody is better than me
- Everything is worthless
- Explosive behavior
- Family "curse" connected with business, finances, health, marriage, etc.
- Fear of being alone
- Fear of burglars breaking into house
- Fear of change/the unknown
- Fear of driving after dark

- Fear of driving on freeways/highways
- Fear of flying
- Fear of intimacy
- Fear of job interviews
- Fear of new people/places
- Fear of nighttime
- Fear of sleeping alone
- Fear of success
- Fear of the darks
- Feel invisible throughout my life
- Feel like a failure
- Feel people only tolerate me
- Feel threatened to ask for a raise
- Fighting/wrestling with my demons
- Financial struggles
- Fly off the handle quickly
- Forgetting how to throw a baseball
- Freaked out over expectations and competition at school or work
- Friends and relationships that exhaust me
- Frustration
- Gossiping fallout
- Grieving years after a loss
- Guilt
- Habitually late
- Habituated to surfing porn
- Haunted by a memory
- Haunted by deepest fear
- Health issues
- Helpless
- High maintenance friends or relationships
- Holiday blues
- Holiday stress
- Hopeless

- Humiliation/embarrassment
- Hypercritical
- Ignoring red flags while on a date
- Incarcerated
- I'm my worst critic/enemy
- Infidelity
- Illness upon retirement
- Incessant mental chatter
- Indecisive
- Insecure
- Intimidated by _____
- Invalidated by _____
- Irritability
- Jealousy
- Judgmental
- Lazy
- Let things bug me/get to me
- Lying a lot
- Life is unfair
- Loneliness
- Low self-esteem/self-worth
- Made fun of by _____
- Made to feel it's all my fault by _____
- Made to feel whatever I do is never good enough for _____
- Mental block
- Mid-life crisis
- Miscarried but never grieved
- Morbid thoughts
- Mothering/fathering issues
- Motivational blocks
- My child stopped speaking with me
- My child won't let me see my grandchild
- Naive/Gullible

- Need for approval
- Need to be right all the time
- Need to lighten up
- Negative thoughts
- Neglecting myself
- Nervous
- Never acknowledged
- Never did anything right in my life
- Never enough time
- Never good enough
- Never got acknowledgement
- Never grieved for a particular person
- Never truly happy
- Nightmares
- No direction in my life
- No energy
- No "real" friends
- Not following through
- Obnoxious people
- Obsessing
- Only find losers
- Only loved for my money/status
- Overeating
- People-pleaser
- People who press my buttons
- Perfectionist
- Performance anxiety
- Performer's anxiety over auditions/call backs
- Personal demons
- Pessimistic
- Pet peeve
- Phantom pains
- Physical fear of men/women

- Picking wrong partners
- Pregnancy and fears
- Prejudice
- Pressure from self/others' expectations
- Procrastinate
- Quit one addiction, add/increase another
- Rage
- Regrets
- Rejection
- Resentment
- Road rage
- Sabotage myself
- Sadness
- Second-guessing
- Self-doubt
- Self-critical
- Shame/blame
- Short fuse
- Shy
- Sleeping issues
- Sleeping with your cell phone
- Social misfit
- Social anxiety/discomfort
- Some worry is always in the back of my mind
- Something holds me back
- Something makes me _____
- Sports mental blocks
- Sports anxiety
- Still not over relationship/divorce/loss
- Stress associated with _____
- Struggle raising my child/children
- Stuck/trapped
- Superiority

- Take things personally
- Test anxiety
- Tragic death/suicide in family or circle of friends
- Trust issues
- Unable to find a good mate
- Unable to have eye contact
- Unhappy
- Upsetting emotional feelings associated with medical symptoms, flus, cold, etc.
- Uptight
- Urges
- Verbal abuse
- Victim/martyr
- Void in my life
- Waiting for the other shoe to drop
- Wedding jitters/cold feet
- Withdrawing
- Workaholic/Driven/Type A
- Worried about aging
- Worried about my child's being bullied
- Worried about my students' being bullied
- Worried about "What ifs"
- Worry over losing hair
- Writer's/artist's blocks
- Your smartphone gets more time than you give your children
- Your child's going through something you experienced as a child

Appendix B

Applications of Imagine All Better

"Logic will get you from A to B. Imagination will take you everywhere."

— Albert Einstein

Imagine All Better offers you solutions not only to your life, but also to those with whom you come in contact. Individuals who perform the following functions can use this process to bring benefit to those they encounter in their work:

Teachers can bring calm to students who have difficulty focusing or who come to school with turmoil issues.

Students can reduce the anxiety that accompanies test-taking and public speaking.

Creative people such as artists and writers who have developed a mental block can remove them.

Parents can use the technique on their children and each other to reduce stress in their family.

Doctors, dentists, nurses and other healthcare professionals along with support staff can reduce patients' fear and anxiety that normally accompanies patients seeking medical care. This approach can be effective in reducing a patient's blood pressure and anxiety associated with examination procedures, fear of syringes, etc.

Law enforcement officers can remove patterns that cause impulsive overreactions in confrontations.

Professionals who treat rape victims, sexual-assault and trauma victims may calm the victims' emotional feelings immediately.

People ordered to attend anger management classes can benefit from the class leaders using the technique to remove the anger associated with the situation that led to the anger-management requirement. The result of using the technique benefits not only to the persons themselves, but also their spouses, significant others and children.

Suicide hotline counselors can decrease callers' levels of depression, sadness and anger.

Ambulance drivers and paramedics can effortlessly use the technique dealing with the fear and anxiety their patient is having as they drive to the hospital.

Counselors can use the technique with employees who are traumatized at work by a robbery, accident or a violent act.

Mental health professionals can use it as an adjunct to help their clients to remove upsetting emotions and allow their clients to focus on their issues more effectively.

Workers who provide telephone service such as computer help, reservation assistance or emergency dispatch can reduce tensions in their callers.

People who resolve complaints from customers can help to calm them down and reduce their own stress at work.

Coaches and sports psychologists can help athletes remove anxiety, judgmental and critical inner chatter, second-guessing and self-doubt, fear and tension throughout their body that hinders athletic performance.

Clergy members can reduce the intensity of troubling emotions in those whom they counsel.

Post traumatic stress syndrome victims can benefit by removing repeating and crippling emotions associated with their original trauma.

Emergency rooms can address both the physical and emotionally related issues simultaneously.

Mediators can use the technique in helping to resolve disputes by defusing the emotions that the disputing parties bring to mediation.

Prisoners can use the technique to manage their anger and destroy the patterns that got them into prison.

Body workers such as masseurs, masseuses, and physical therapists can use the technique as an adjunct to their practices.

www.ingramcontent.com/pod-product-compliance
Lightning Source LLC
Chambersburg PA
CBHW031347040426
42444CB00005B/218